_____

Presented To

_____

Presented By

_____

Date

Jesus said, "You are like light for the whole world. A city built on top of a hill cannot be hidden."

Matthew 5:14 CEV

IN His OWN WORDS

Jesus said, "Ask, and
it will be given to you;
seek, and you will
find; knock, and it will
be opened to you."

Matthew 7:7 NASB

In His Own Words

WORDS

MEDITATIONS
ON THE
WORDS OF JESUS

BETHANY HOUSE

Minneapolis, Minnesota

In His Own Words
Copyright © 2004 by GRQ Ink, Inc.
Franklin, Tennessee 37067

Published by Bethany House Publishers
11400 Hampshire Avenue South
Bloomington, Minnesota 55438
www.bethanyhouse.com

Bethany House Publishers is a Division of Baker Book House Company, Grand Rapids, Michigan.

Library of Congress Control Number 2003017206.
ISBN 0-7642-2865-X

Compiler and Editor: Lila Empson
Manuscript written by Alton Gansky
Design: Whisner Design Group

04 05 06   4 3 2 1

Simon Peter answered Him, "Lord, to whom shall we go? You have words of eternal life."

John 6:68 NIV

Contents

Introduction

"Heaven and earth
will pass away, but
My words will not
pass away"

Matthew 24:35 NASB

Jesus uttered these words nearly two thousand
years ago. Time has proven Jesus' point. No matter how much time passes, no matter how nations
rise and fall, the teachings of Christ reverberate
through the world undiminished and undiluted.
Each new generation has the opportunity to
experience them as if Jesus had uttered them
only moments before.

Jesus painted with a wide brush. His teachings,
comments, parables, sermons, admonishments,
and more could move multitudes numbered in
the tens of thousands or touch a single life.

What follows is a tribute to the life-changing words of Christ, words that have lifted trampled egos, soothed anxious minds, quieted trembling hearts, inspired noble aspirations, and taught truth that cannot be tarnished by eons of spent years.

There is freshness in the words of Christ. Centuries ago his words made a difference—they make a difference today. Countless thousands have found more than they could imagine in the teaching of Christ. So can you.

Here is truth, in his own words.

Making Life's Heart Choices

Jesus said, "Do not let
your heart be troubled,
nor let it be fearful."

John 14:27 NASB

The Story Behind What Jesus Said

The Upper Room was filled with darkness and tension.
A follower named Judas had turned traitor; his plan was
already in motion. The interval between these words and
Jesus' death on the cross could be counted in mere hours.

Jesus was moving closer to his destiny. In the midst of that
heartrending betrayal, Jesus offered comfort to his faithful
disciples. Jesus spoke of his death, and such words were
difficult for his followers to hear. Emotions stirred within
them: confusion, uncertainty, fear—fear could not be
ignored. What could they do? Jesus told them they had a
choice about how fear affected their hearts. The disciples
learned they could make the "heart" choices; and heart
choices made all the difference.

Reflections on the Words of Jesus

During your life your heart will beat over two billion times. To the doctor, the heart is a pump; to the poet, a metaphor for love; to the people of Jesus' day, the center of emotion and reason.

Hearts can be troublesome. Early on one learns that the heart can hurt. A harsh word or unexpected tragedy can make your heart ache.

Jesus taught that you are responsible for your heart and that you choose how you respond. He didn't say "avoid the hurt" or "deny the pain." He gave a command: "Do not let not your heart be troubled." There is power in that command, a freedom to evict worry, eject concern, and embrace peace. The choice is yours. Every day you can say, "I choose not to worry; I choose not to fear. That is my 'heart choice.'"

One Final Thought

You have been given the power to make life's heart choices. You have the privilege of trusting Jesus with your fears and anxieties.

Timeless Wisdom for Everyday Living

Making Life's Heart Choices

There is no fear in love; but perfect love casts out fear, because fear involves punishment, and the one who fears is not perfected in love.
1 John 4:18 NASB

Jesus said, Blessed are the pure in heart: for they shall see God.
Matthew 5:8 KJV

Pray about everything. . . . If you do this, you will experience God's peace, which is far more wonderful than the human mind can understand. His peace will guard your hearts and minds as you live in Christ Jesus.
Philippians 4:6-7 NLT

Joshua said to the Israelites, "Have I not commanded you? Be strong and courageous. Do not be terrified; do not be discouraged, for the LORD your God will be with you wherever you go."
Joshua 1:9 NIV

Trust in him at all times; ye people, pour out your heart before him: God is a refuge for us. Selah.
Psalm 62:8 KJV

Anxiety in a man's heart weighs it down, but a good word makes it glad. Proverbs 12:25 NASB

No passion so effectually robs the mind of all its powers of acting and reasoning as fear.
Edmund Burke

Courage is not simply one of the virtues but the form of every virtue at the testing point, which means at the point of highest reality.
C. S. Lewis

Brave men are all vertebrates; they have their softness on the surface and their toughness in the middle.
G. K. Chesterton

Courage is resistance to fear, mastery of fear—not absence of fear.
Mark Twain

A mighty fortress is our God; a bulwark never failing. Martin Luther

Courage is the price that Life exacts for granting peace, the soul that knows it not, knows no release from little things.
Amelia Earhart

It is only when we do know Him that we are not afraid, for there is nothing to fear.
Peter Marshall

Rustproofing Your Treasure

Jesus said, "Store up for yourselves treasures in heaven, where moth and rust do not destroy, and where thieves do not break in and steal. For where your treasure is, there your heart will be also."

Matthew 6:20–21 NIV

The Story Behind What Jesus Said

It was a large crowd; people were hungering to hear words that would make a difference in their lives. They left homes and jobs to go to a mountain to hear the Man everyone was talking about. They were not disappointed. Using just the power of his voice and a charisma that could not be ignored, Jesus laid out practical truth for everyday living. He spoke of relationships, prayer, and even financial matters.

On the grassy hill, Jesus brought a unique teaching to these matters. Those around him were concerned with meeting the day's needs and acquiring tomorrow's wealth. Jesus spoke of riches with eternal value; he spoke of treasures that were not subject to the destructive forces of this world.

People spend a lot of energy acquiring the necessary "treasure" to live. You work hard, you save, and you count what you have. The things you value become your treasures.

Your riches can be art, precious stones, or valuable metals like gold and silver. Whatever form they take, however, they are all subject to the forces of nature. They deteriorate, rust, and corrode; at the very least, they remain earthbound. Jesus spoke of a different treasure, one built by faith; he spoke of a treasure more secure than the gold in Fort Knox.

The treasure that lasts is work done for God and on his behalf. How do you build an eternal, rustproof treasure? By expressing the love of God in all that you do and say. Each kindness done in God's name builds a treasure that is indestructible and a wealth you will enjoy in this life and the next.

One Final Thought

Your most important treasure won't fit in a safety-deposit box, but it will fit in your heart. Build on faith and invest in love.

Rustproofing Your Treasure

For riches do not last forever, nor a crown for all generations. Proverbs 27:24 NRSV

Do not trust in extortion or take pride in stolen goods; though your riches increase, do not set your heart on them.
Psalm 62:10 NIV

Those who desire to be rich fall into temptation and a snare, and into many foolish and harmful lusts which drown men in destruction and perdition. For the love of money is a root of all kinds of evil.
1 Timothy 6:9–10a NKJV

You cannot be a slave of two masters; you will hate one and love the other; you will be loyal to one and despise the other. You cannot serve both God and money.
Matthew 6:24 GNT

Our LORD Jesus Christ was kind enough to give up all his riches and become poor, so that you could become rich.
2 Corinthians 8:9 CEV

Riches are sometimes hoarded to the harm of the saver. Ecclesiastes 5:13 NLT

Even the rich are hungry for love, for being cared for, for being wanted, for having someone to call their own.
Mother Teresa

Indeed, if we consider the unblushing promises of reward and the staggering nature of the rewards promised in the Gospels, it would seem that our Lord finds our desires not too strong, but too weak.
C. S. Lewis

The main emotion of the adult American who has had all the advantages of wealth, education, and culture is disappointment.
John Cheever

Take my silver and my gold, not a mite would I withhold; take my moments and my days, let them flow in ceaseless praise.
Frances R. Havergal

Prosperity is only an instrument to be used, not a deity to be worshiped.
Calvin Coolidge

There's a fundamental connection between our spiritual lives and how we think about and handle money. We may try to divorce our faith and our finances, but God sees them as inseparable.
Randy Alcorn

A Diet That Makes a Difference

Jesus said, "People need more than bread for their life; they must feed on every word of God."

Matthew 4:4 NLT

The Story Behind What Jesus Said

Before he uttered these words, Jesus had been standing in the Jordan River having just been baptized in its cool waters. The Bible describes the Holy Spirit descending upon Jesus and the voice of God booming from heaven, "This is my beloved Son, in whom I am well pleased."

From that high point, Jesus was led into the wilderness to be tempted. Alone in the desolation, Jesus endured severe hunger and the elements. No admiring crowds, no voices from heaven—just temptations. Days of fasting had taken their toll. Hunger gnawed at him. The devil suggested that Jesus turn stones into bread. But there was more at stake than easing hunger pains; there was the matter of obedience to God.

The word *diet* is heard more today than at any other time in history. Bookstores are filled with every imaginable type of diet, each book promising certain and absolute success.

There is a part of you that meat and potatoes can't feed; it is that immaterial part called the soul. Like the body, it grows hungry. The soul must be fed or it grows weak and you grow feeble. The soul has a special diet. What do you feed your soul? Jesus provided the answer.

Your soul is meant to feast on the words of God. When you listen to him, when you read his word, you start a diet healthy for the spirit, a diet that has eternal ramifications. God has spoken with words meant for your ears. Those words have been recorded in the Bible. They are words you can and should consume every day. It is the diet that makes a difference.

One Final Thought

Each day brings a new and needed opportunity to consume the truth that can be found in God's Word, the Bible. Feast on it every day.

Do not merely listen to the word, and so deceive yourselves. Do what it says. James 1:22 NIV

Be diligent to present yourself approved to God as a workman who does not need to be ashamed, accurately handling the word of truth.

2 Timothy 2:15 NASB

Remember what Christ taught and let his words enrich your lives and make you wise; teach them to each other and sing them out in psalms and hymns and spiritual songs, singing to the LORD with thankful hearts.

Colossians 3:16 TLB

God means what he says. What he says goes. His powerful Word is sharp as a surgeon's scalpel, cutting through everything, whether doubt or defense, laying us open to listen and obey.

Hebrews 4:12 THE MESSAGE

These were more fair-minded than those in Thessalonica, in that they received the word with all readiness, and searched the Scriptures daily to find out whether these things were so.

Acts 17:11 NKJV

Jesus replied, "But even more blessed are all who hear the word of God and put it into practice." Luke 11:28 NLT

I have for many years made it a practice to read through the Bible once a year. My custom is to read four or five chapters every morning immediately after rising from my bed. It employs about an hour of my time, and seems to me the most suitable manner of beginning the day.
John Quincy Adams

To read the Bible is to take a trip to a fair land where the spirit is strengthened and faith renewed.
Dwight D. Eisenhower

The New Testament is the very best book that ever was or ever will be known in the world.
Charles Dickens

My ground is the Bible. I follow it in all things, both great and small.
John Wesley

I believe the Bible is the best gift God has ever given to man. All the good from the Savior of the world is communicated to us through this book.
Abraham Lincoln

Believe me, sir, never a night goes by, be I ever so tired, but I read the Word of God before I go to bed.
Douglas MacArthur

23

How to Get Rid of Darkness

Jesus said, "You are like light for the whole world. A city built on top of a hill cannot be hidden."

Matthew 5:14 CEV

The Story Behind What Jesus Said

In the land of Jesus, light came from only a few sources: cooking fires, torches, or ceramic lamps. Lamps were made by hand, crafted from clay. Household lamps often were little more than bowls filled with olive oil in which floated a wick made of flax. Other lamps looked similar to small teapots, the lighted wick extending from the spout.

In Jesus' day, light was important. Electricity was unknown and the light bulb was two thousand years in the future. People who lived then understood darkness. They also understood that a tiny clay lamp held in the palm of the hand could push back darkness. That day on that hillside, some learned that they had the same power.

Over your head flickers a bejeweled sky, seen only at night. Here is one of the great ironies of life: the darker the night, the brighter the stars.

Darkness has no substance, but it can feel heavy and oppressive. Unwanted darkness is persistent. It cannot be swept from your life, vacuumed away, or tucked in a corner. The only way to get rid of darkness is to introduce light.

Jesus' words are a reminder that you are a light of the world. Just as the night sky is tempered by the many stars that shine in it, so you too contribute your light to the world. Sometimes you need someone else's light; other times they need yours. Fragile as you are, your light can still put darkness in its place. What is your light? It is every kind word, every wrong forgiven, every bit of wisdom shared and love expressed. Darkness cannot overcome the light that blazes out of you.

One Final Thought

You are the light of the world and your glow can push back any darkness. Share your light. Combine your light with others and watch the darkness flee.

Your word is a lamp to my feet and a light to my path. Psalm 119:105 NKJV

Don't hide your light! Let it shine for all; let your good deeds glow for all to see, so that they will praise your heavenly Father.
Matthew 5:15–16 TLB

Do everything without complaining or arguing, so that you may become blameless and pure, children of God without fault in a crooked and depraved generation, in which you shine like stars in the universe.
Philippians 2:14–15 NIV

If we walk in the light as He is in the light, we have fellowship with one another, and the blood of Jesus Christ His Son cleanses us from all sin.
1 John 1:7 NKJV

For once you were darkness, but now in the LORD you are light. Live as children of light.
Ephesians 5:8 NRSV

You are all children of the light and of the day; we don't belong to darkness and night.
1 Thessalonians 5:5 NLT

From a little spark may burst a mighty flame.
Dante Alighieri

At times our own light goes out and is rekindled by a spark from another person. Each of us has cause to think with deep gratitude of those who have lighted the flame within us.
Albert Schweitzer

How far that little candle throws his beams! So shines a good deed in a naughty world.
William Shakespeare

The true division of humanity is between those who live in light and those who live in darkness.
Victor Hugo

I'd rather light a candle than curse the darkness. James Kelly

We are told to let our light shine, and if it does, we won't need to tell anybody it does. Lighthouses don't fire cannons to call attention to their shining—they just shine.
Dwight L. Moody

Showing Worry the Door

Jesus said, "So don't worry about tomorrow, for tomorrow will bring its own worries. Today's trouble is enough for today."

Matthew 6:34 NLT

The Story Behind What Jesus Said

Worry is not new. Those who lived in Jesus' day were well acquainted with the ogre called worry. Jesus never dodged the hard issues, and he didn't duck the thing that afflicted the hundreds who had come to hear him.

Looking at the crowd, Jesus saw scores of faces creased with the lasting lines of worry. They worried then as people do now. Would there be enough food for the kids? Why is business bad? What happens to the family if I die? Most of these people were commoners, hardworking, family-loving, regular folk who struggled to make ends meet, rear a family, serve God, and find happiness. Jesus gave them pointed advice: "Stop worrying about tomorrow. Deal with today."

To be human is to experience worry; to experience worry is to dilute happiness. God did not create you to be a vessel filled with worry, but somehow it comes anyway. The things that cause worry form an endless list. It is because worry is so prevalent that Jesus taught that you can choose a worry-free life.

That is not to say that your concerns are not real; nor does it mean that you should avoid responsibility for the challenges in your life. Jesus merely meant that worry is a useless emotional effort that can only harm and never betters.

Today's problems need to be addressed, but churning up anxiety about tomorrow achieves nothing. Face your problems and do what must be done, but don't give in to worry. Worry is not a solution, it's an additional problem. Deal with today's troubles today. Let go of worry, seize determined action, and have faith in God for the rest.

One Final Thought

Worry has never changed anything; faith changes everything. Show useless worry the way out of your life, and never invite it back in. Then face the challenge before you.

Cast your burden upon the LORD and He will sustain you; He will never allow the righteous to be shaken. Psalm 55:22 NASB

An anxious heart weighs a man down, but a kind word cheers him up.
Proverbs 12:25 NIV

Peace I leave with you; my peace I give you. I do not give to you as the world gives. Do not let your hearts be troubled and do not be afraid.
John 14:27 NIV

Rest in the LORD; wait patiently for him to act. Don't be envious of evil men who prosper. Stop your anger! Turn off your wrath. Don't fret and worry—it only leads to harm.
Psalm 37:7–8 TLB

Humble yourselves under the mighty power of God, and in his good time he will honor you. Give all your worries and cares to God, for he cares about what happens to you.
1 Peter 5:6–7 NLT

Having food and clothing, with these we shall be content. 1 Timothy 6:8 NKJV

The beginning of anxiety is the end of faith. The beginning of true faith is the end of anxiety.
George Müller

"Worry" is a word that I don't allow myself to use.
Dwight D. Eisenhower

Worry often gives a small thing a big shadow.
Swedish Proverb

Blessed is the man who is too busy to worry in the daytime and too sleepy to worry at night.
Phil Marquart

Worry, like a rocking chair, will give you something to do, but it won't get you anywhere. Vance Havner

A problem not worth praying about is not worth worrying about.
Anonymous

It only seems as if you are doing something when you're worrying.
Lucy Maud Montgomery

The Knock That Makes a Difference

Jesus said, "Ask, and it will be given to you; seek, and you will find; knock, and it will be opened to you."

Matthew 7:7 NASB

The Story Behind What Jesus Said

Much of Jesus' teaching was startling. Old concepts became new; dim ideas shone with new brightness. So it was with his teaching about prayer. Before Jesus uttered these words, he taught the Lord's Prayer. It was as a template, elements that make prayer meaningful and powerful. He taught that God not only listened to the prayers of his children, but he also eagerly welcomed them. The crowd needed to know their prayers were not an inconvenience to God.

So Jesus taught them to be bold. *Ask, seek,* and *knock* are more than just words; they are the pattern of prayer. Jesus wanted the congregation to know that they could ask, seek, and knock on God's door about any matter that concerned them.

No one wants to be a bother. It is part of human nature to apologize when making a request of someone. For many, that includes requests made of God. That's the wrong approach. It is God's desire, his pleasure, his joy to hear from his children. No apologies are necessary to begin a conversation with the Creator.

The New Testament was written in an ancient form of Greek in which words carry more meaning than they do in English. The way Jesus said this implied persistence: keep asking, keep seeking, and keep knocking. Not once. Not twice, but frequently—daily. That day, the crowd learned that God has willing ears and is not annoyed by repeated requests.

Ask, seek, knock—powerful words, words of freedom, hope, and acceptance. These are words that open doors of communication with God. The key is persistence. Keep on asking. Keep on seeking. Keep on knocking. That is how prayer should be done.

One Final Thought

God never says, "What? You again?" Instead, he leans forward to hear the words of his children. He is eager to hear from you every day, so speak up.

Turn to the LORD! He can still be found. Call out to God! He is near. Isaiah 55:6 CEV

I urge, then, first of all, that requests, prayers, intercession and thanksgiving be made for everyone. . . . I want men everywhere to lift up holy hands in prayer.

1 Timothy 2:1, 8a NIV

We are sure of this, that he will listen to us whenever we ask him for anything in line with his will. And if we really know he is listening when we talk to him and make our requests, then we can be sure that he will answer us.

1 John 5:14–15 TLB

Confess your sins to each other and pray for each other so that you may be healed. The earnest prayer of a righteous person has great power and wonderful results.

James 5:16 NLT

Continue in prayer, and watch in the same with thanksgiving.

Colossians 4:2 KJV

O You who hear prayer, to You all flesh will come. Psalm 65:2 NKJV

My prayers seem to be more of an attitude than anything else. I indulge in no lip service, but ask the great God silently, daily, and often many times a day, to permit me to speak to Him. I ask Him to give me wisdom, understanding and bodily strength to do His will. Hence, I am asking and receiving all the time.
George Washington Carver

Prayer takes the mind out of the narrowness of self-interest, and enables us to see the world in the mirror of the holy.
Abraham Joshua Heschel

Prayer is not overcoming God's reluctance, it is laying hold of His highest willingness.
Richard C. Trench

More things are wrought by prayer than this world dreams of.

Alfred, Lord Tennyson

Prayer does not change God, but it changes him who prays.
Søren Kierkegaard

Groanings which cannot be uttered are often prayers which cannot be refused.
C. H. Spurgeon

Taking the Oops Out

Jesus said, "No one puts a patch of unshrunk cloth on an old garment. . . . Nor do people put new wine into old wineskins . . . but they put new wine into fresh wineskins, and both are preserved."

Matthew 9:16–17 NASB

The Story Behind What Jesus Said

John's disciples asked a pressing question, "Why do we and the Pharisees fast, but your disciples do not fast?" Jesus and his disciples were feasting, not fasting, and people wanted to know why. The answer came in a two-part illustration. Cloth in Jesus' time shrank after being washed. Every homemaker knew that patching an old garment with a new piece of material was a sure way to make a bigger hole. The same was true of wineskins. New wine was placed in the goatskin "bottle" and it would expand as wine fermented. Putting new wine in an already stretched wineskin would soon cause it to burst.

Jesus brought something new, something that would stretch the existing system to the breaking point.

When architects design skyscrapers they do so with an unusual goal: they make the building flexible. The taller the structure, the more flexible it needs to be. To create a massive tower of concrete and steel that refuses to budge is to invite disaster. It was a lesson hard learned. So architects and engineers design their buildings to move in an earthquake or strong wind. A swaying building is stronger than a rigid building. The same can be said of people.

Encountering Jesus changes you. Learning his words causes you to stretch your thinking, your emotions, and your actions. This is frightening for some people, who make themselves inflexible and rigid to resist change. Other people embrace change gladly.

Change is part of life and should be embraced as something that makes you better. This is certainly true with the teaching of Jesus. Rigidity harms; flexibility leads to strength.

One Final Thought

Whatever has made you rigid to change in the past needs to be replaced by the flexibility of a life placed in Christ.

Create in me a pure heart, O God, and renew a steadfast spirit within me.
Psalm 51:10 NIV

Take on an entirely new way of life—a God-fashioned life, a life renewed from the inside and working itself into your conduct as God accurately reproduces his character in you.
Ephesians 4:22b–24 THE MESSAGE

Jesus replied, "I assure you, unless you are born again, you can never see the Kingdom of God. . . . No one can enter the Kingdom of God without being born of water and the Spirit."
John 3:3, 5 NLT

"Then I will give them one heart, and I will put a new spirit within them . . . and they shall be My people, and I will be their God."
Ezekiel 11:19–20 NKJV

We are what he has made us, created in Christ Jesus for good works, which God prepared beforehand to be our way of life.
Ephesians 2:10 NRSV

Anyone who belongs to Christ is a new person. The past is forgotten, and everything is new. 2 Corinthians 5:17 CEV

Everybody thinks of changing humanity and nobody thinks of changing himself.
Leo Tolstoy

Would that life were like the shadow cast by a wall or a tree, but it is like the shadow of a bird in flight.
The Talmud

The old order changeth yielding place to new, and God fulfills Himself in many ways.
Alfred, Lord Tennyson

All things must change to something new, to something strange.
Henry Wadsworth Longfellow

We all change, whether we like it or not. Ralph Waldo Emerson

God, grant me the serenity to accept the things I cannot change, the courage to change the things I can, and the wisdom to know the difference.
Reinhold Niebuhr

Christians are supposed not merely to endure change, nor even to profit by it, but to cause it.
Harry Emerson Fosdick

39

The Rest Stop

Jesus said, "Come to Me, all who are weary and heavy–laden, and I will give you rest."
Matthew 11:28 NASB

The Story Behind What Jesus Said

Weariness was as much a part of life in Jesus' day as it is now. People bore the burdens of work, family, finances, political oppression, and health. The people to whom Jesus spoke bore another burden—a crushing religious burden. The weight didn't come from God, but from years of reinterpreting what God had commanded. Added to God's laws were human laws that dictated every detail of life. Sadly, laws meant to honor God grew into laws that obscured him.

Jesus offered something different, not a long laundry list of do's and don'ts, but a pattern of living that not only honored God but freed the individual to experience the vast abundance of the spiritual life.

The Great Pyramid of Giza towers fifty stories above the Egyptian sand. It was constructed from over two million blocks, some of which weighed as much as fifteen metric tons. Such buildings cannot be made without learning to deal with crushing weight. Today we build with cranes and heavy equipment, some of which are as large as a house.

There is another type of weight that cannot be handled with pulleys, forklifts, or cranes—the weight of life. Some of these burdens come from others or just from life; sometimes people weigh themselves down.

Jesus offered to help. He did so by invitation. Jesus doesn't take the weight from your shoulders without your permission. He does so only when you take your burden to him. In prayer lay your burdens down before Jesus. You will be able to stand straighter, move freer, and breathe easier than you ever thought possible. Jesus is waiting to hear from you.

One Final Thought

Jesus didn't bring new burdens, but a new rest, and he did it with an open invitation to everyone—including you.

I can do all things through Christ who strengthens me. Philippians 4:13 NKJV

Christ has freed us so that we may enjoy the benefits of freedom. Therefore, be firm [in this freedom], and don't become slaves again.

Galatians 5:1 GOD'S WORD

Those who wait on the LORD will find new strength. They will fly high on wings like eagles. They will run and not grow weary. They will walk and not faint.

Isaiah 40:31 NLT

This is love for God: to obey his commands. And his commands are not burdensome, for everyone born of God overcomes the world. This is the victory that has overcome the world, even our faith.

1 John 5:3–4 NIV

Return, O my soul, to your rest, for the LORD has dealt bountifully with you.

Psalm 116:7 NRSV

Some will come to me—those the Father has given me—and I will never, never reject them. John 6:37 TLB

I heard the voice of Jesus say, "Come unto Me and rest; lay down, thou weary one, lay down thy head upon My breast." I came to Jesus as I was, weary and worn and sad; I found in Him a resting place, and He has made me glad.

Horatius Bonar

Days are filled with sorrow and care; hearts are heavy and drear; burdens are lifted at Calvary—Jesus is very near.

John M. Moore

There is a place of full release, near to the heart of God, a place where all is joy and peace, near to the heart of God.

Cleland B. McAfee

Whate'er we leave to God, God does and blesses us.

Henry David Thoreau

Jesus, I am resting, resting in the joy of what Thou art; I am finding out the greatness of Thy loving heart. Thou hast bid me gaze upon Thee, and Thy beauty fills my soul, for by Thy transforming power Thou hast made me whole.

Jean Sophia Pigott

Doing a Good Thing

He said to them, "What man is there among you who has a sheep, and if it falls into a pit on the Sabbath, will he not take hold of it and lift it out?"

Matthew 12:11 NASB

The Story Behind What Jesus Said

Jesus was beleaguered by a group of legalistic religious leaders called Pharisees. The requirements they added to God's Law were burdensome and at times ridiculous. A tailor couldn't carry a needle on the Sabbath! One Sabbath, Jesus entered a local synagogue and found a man with a crippled hand. The Pharisees pressed Jesus, "Is it lawful to heal on the Sabbath?" Since healing would be considered work, the expected answer was no.

Saving an animal from harm was allowable. It appeared that farm animals were more important than people. Jesus responded with a question of his own. If they had concern for an animal, shouldn't he have more concern for a human? Without lifting a finger, Jesus healed the afflicted man.

Every year, somewhere in the world, people can view a solar eclipse. As the moon passes in front of the sun a shadow is cast on the earth. From earth's perspective, the moon blots out the entire face of the sun. In a total eclipse, things can get pretty dark.

Legalism—making laws more important than God—is similar, blotting out the truth in favor of rules. Too often the regulations become more important than the people they were meant to guide. It's an old problem, one that Jesus had to deal with often.

Jesus is more interested in people—in you—than in a set of rules. Jesus is the great liberator. Righteousness, he taught, was not in a code of rules but action motivated by love. Goodness is described not by "I don't do this," but in the good that you do in Jesus' name. Jesus never missed an opportunity to do what was beneficial to others. Neither should you.

One Final Thought

When life gives you the opportunity to do good for others, you should follow Jesus' example and do it. Any day—today, for example—is a great day to start.

Timeless Wisdom for Everyday Living

Doing a Good Thing

It's criminal to ignore a neighbor in need, but compassion for the poor—what a blessing!

Proverbs 14:21 THE MESSAGE

Rejoice with those who rejoice; mourn with those who mourn.

Romans 12:15 NIV

Love is patient and kind. Love is not jealous or boastful or proud or rude. Love does not demand its own way. Love is not irritable, and it keeps no record of when it has been wronged.

1 Corinthians 13:4–5 NLT

We then who are strong ought to bear with the scruples of the weak, and not to please ourselves. Let each of us please his neighbor for his good, leading to edification.

Romans 15:1–2 NKJV

Bear one another's burdens, and in this way you will fulfill the law of Christ.

Galatians 6:2 NRSV

Friend, don't go along with evil. Model the good. The person who does good does God's work. The person who does evil falsifies God, doesn't know the first thing about God. 3 John 1:11 THE MESSAGE

To ease another's heartache
is to forget one's own.
Abraham Lincoln

In the time we have it is
surely our duty to do all
the good we can to all the
people we can in all the
ways we can.
William Barclay

O God, when I am wrong,
make me easy to change,
and when I am right,
make me easy to live with!
Peter Marshall

When you are good to oth-
ers, you are best to yourself.
Ben Franklin

He who does not live in some degree for others, hardly lives for himself.
Michel de Montaigne

Do all the good you can,
By all the means you can,
In all the ways you can,
In all the places you can,
At all the times you can,
To all the people you can,
As long as ever you can.
John Wesley

Life becomes harder for
us when we live for oth-
ers, but it also becomes
richer and happier.
Albert Schweitzer

Defeating the Divide

Knowing their thoughts Jesus said to them, "Any kingdom divided against itself is laid waste; and any city or house divided against itself will not stand."

Matthew 12:25 NASB

The Story Behind What Jesus Said

Standing before Jesus was a man who had three hard strikes against him. He was blind, mute, and possessed by a demon. Still he had some friends who led him to Jesus. Jesus wasted no time in casting out the demon, healing eyes that had ceased to work, and freeing the tongue that had never spoken.

The crowd was impressed and began to ask if Jesus was the Son of David, a reference to his being the long-awaited Messiah. When Jesus' enemies heard this praise, they snapped back, "This man casts out demons by the ruler of demons." In other words, Satan. Their logic was critically flawed, and Jesus made that clear. A kingdom divided against itself cannot stand.

Jesus was the only person to live a perfect and sinless life. Still his enemies created reasons to be critical. Even in the face of great healing miracles, his adversaries used the sharpest words and the most cutting remarks to turn people against him. Many of the greatest lessons for life came from these confrontations.

On June 16, 1858, Abraham Lincoln used Jesus' words to highlight the danger of a nation split over slavery. The logic was undeniable. Division is always damaging. It is true for countries, families, individuals, and people's own minds. Unity is strength; harmony is powerful. This is true for groups and it is also true for the internal conflict people often feel.

The divide of heart and mind must be defeated, and Jesus stands ready to help, just as he stood ready to heal a man with three crippling strikes against him. Seek unity of mind, of family, of business, of your spiritual life.

One Final Thought

A divided mind and heart is a slick slope, but a determined and unswerving person stands stronger than all others. Division can be healed.

If you are guided by the Spirit, you won't obey your selfish desires. Galatians 5:16 CEV

Let us therefore make every effort to do what leads to peace and to mutual edification.
Romans 4:19 NIV

I beg you in the name of the LORD Jesus Christ to stop arguing among yourselves. Let there be real harmony so that there won't be splits in the church. I plead with you to be of one mind, united in thought and purpose.
1 Corinthians 1:10 TLB

Whatever happens, conduct yourselves in a manner worthy of the gospel of Christ. Then, whether I come and see you or only hear about you in my absence, I will know that you stand firm in one spirit, contending as one man for the faith of the gospel
Philippians 1:27 NIV

See how good and pleasant it is when brothers and sisters live together in harmony!
Psalm 133:1 GOD'S WORD

Depart from evil, and do good; seek peace, and pursue it. Psalm 34:14 NRSV

To be free from evil
thoughts is God's
best gift.
Aeschylus of Eleusis

A Christian is a person
who thinks in believing
and believes in thinking.
Saint Augustine

Change your
thoughts and you
change your world.
Norman Vincent Peale

It is not enough to have a
good mind. The main
thing is to use it well.
René Descartes

The mind is its own place, and in
itself can make a heaven of hell,
a hell of heaven. John Milton

When our journeys leave
us with more questions
than answers, we can
take our doubts to Jesus in
prayer. Then, Jesus—in
his own way and in his
own time—can replace
those doubts with a confident assurance of God's
promises and a peaceful
acceptance of God's will.
Mary Prince

51

Under Lock and Key

Jesus said, "The good man brings out of his good treasure what is good; and the evil man brings out of his evil treasure what is evil."

Matthew 12:35 NASB

The Story Behind What Jesus Said

In many ways, Jesus was a catalyst. According to chemists, a catalyst is something that brings about a reaction without itself being changed. Wherever Jesus went, he encountered scores of people. Most would be attracted to him; some would react negatively. Sometimes it was hard to distinguish the supporters from the detractors. On the outside they all looked the same.

Each person's nature came out in the words they said. While many praised Jesus, some were highly critical, even to the point of violence. No matter how they looked on the outside, their words would eventually reveal what was going on inside. That was Jesus' point. The inner person would be revealed to the outside world. It could be no other way.

Hospitals use a device called a CAT scanner. It's a large X-ray machine that takes thousands of images and within seconds constructs a three-dimensional picture of the patient's body. It allows doctors to look inside the ailing person. Good as the device is, it cannot show a person's inner nature.

Inside everyone is a treasure. It can be a positive, worthwhile treasure, or it can be evil. Whatever you keep as your treasure is shown in the actions you take and the words you use. What is on the inside becomes evident to those on the outside.

You choose the treasure that resides in you. It might be a chest of faith, hope, kindness, or love, or it might contain hatred, fear, and mistrust. Whatever is on the inside will percolate to the top. It can't be helped, but it can be changed. Choose a treasure that is not only valuable to you but is also valuable to those around you.

One Final Thought

The inner treasure governs the outer life.
Accumulate those qualities that are enduring and
life changing, and your life will change accordingly.

Let the words of my mouth and the meditation of my heart be acceptable in Your sight, O Lord, my strength and my Redeemer.

Psalm 19:14 NKJV

As he thinks within himself, so he is. He says to you, "Eat and drink!" But his heart is not with you.

Proverbs 23:7 NASB

You have obeyed with all your heart the new teaching God has given you. Now you are free from sin, your old master, and you have become slaves to your new master, righteousness.

Romans 6:17b–18 NLT

Command them to do good, to be rich in good deeds, and to be generous and willing to share. In this way they will lay up treasure for themselves as a firm foundation for the coming age.

1 Timothy 6:18–19a NIV

What I am eager for is that all the Christians there will be filled with love that comes from pure hearts.

1 Timothy 1:5a TLB

Take care, brothers and sisters, that none of you may have an evil, unbelieving heart that turns away from the living God.

Hebrews 3:12 NRSV

I will govern my life and my thoughts as if the whole world were to see the one, and to read the other. For what does it signify to make anything a secret to neighbor, when to God, who is the Searcher of hearts, all our privacies are open?
Seneca

It is no use walking anywhere to preach unless we preach as we walk.
Saint Francis of Assisi

Just as Jesus found it necessary to sweep the moneychangers from the Temple porch, so we ourselves need a lot of housecleaning.
Dale Evans Rogers

Character is a by-product; it is produced in the great manufacture of daily duty. Woodrow Wilson

A man is what he believes.
Anton Chekhov

If better were within, better would come out.
Thomas Fuller

Respecting Respect

They took offense at Him. But Jesus said to them, "A prophet is not without honor except in his hometown and in his own household."

Matthew 13:57 NASB

The Story Behind What Jesus Said

Nazareth, Jesus' hometown, was a small village with at most two thousand residents. It was there Jesus grew into manhood and practiced the carpentry craft: making wood plows, setting roofs on stone buildings, and building furniture. It was an important job and one that made him well known to his fellow Nazarenes. There was the problem.

Jesus worked miracles and taught with unrivaled authority. The first time he did this, the town's people tried to push him over a cliff (Luke 4:16–29). This time they were impressed but not to the point of belief. They couldn't get beyond the fact that they had watched Jesus grow up and knew his family by name. They rejected the Savior despite all they had seen.

There's an old saying, "Behind every successful man is a surprised mother-in-law." That sentiment applies to more than mothers-in-law—any family member can be critical. Those who know you best tend to remember your weaknesses and failings. Those things seem to be more memorable than your achievements. It's hard for some to accept change in others' lives.

Still, change happens. You can grow in wisdom and ability. You can become more than you've ever been. Even so, there will always be those who will refuse to believe that you can be anything more than what you were. Such things are to be expected, but you must not allow them to hold you back.

Jesus didn't miss a beat. He continued with his earthly ministry unfazed by undeserved criticism and doubt—and so should you. Words of disbelief from others sting, but they only weigh you down as much as you allow them to. Press on. That is how things get done.

One Final Thought

Critics are abundant. Choose to fix your eyes on the worthwhile goal before you and not on the naysayer, and you will find the freedom to change and grow.

Respecting Respect

Let your speech always be with grace, seasoned with salt, that you may know how you ought to answer each one.

Colossians 4:6 NKJV

Fear of the LORD teaches a person to be wise; humility precedes honor.

Proverbs 15:33 NLT

Don't criticize and speak evil about each other, dear brothers.

James 4:11a TLB

Some of you accuse others of doing wrong. But there is no excuse for what you do. When you judge others, you condemn yourselves, because you are guilty of doing the very same things. We know that God is right to judge everyone who behaves in this way.

Romans 2:1–2 CEV

I care very little if I am judged by you or by any human court; indeed, I do not even judge myself. My conscience is clear, but that does not make me innocent. It is the LORD who judges me.

1 Corinthians 4:3–4 NIV

Be devoted to each other like a loving family. Excel in showing respect for each other. Romans 12:10 GOD'S WORD

I care not what others think of what I do, but I care very much about what I think of what I do. That is character!
Theodore Roosevelt

Pay no attention to what the critics say; there has never been set up a state in honor of a critic.
Jean Sibelius

The respect of those you respect is worth more than the applause of the multitude.
Author Unknown

Anyone who proposes to do good must not expect people to roll stones out of his way, but must accept his lot calmly, even if they roll a few more upon it.
Albert Schweitzer

If a dog barks at a hill, will the hill crumble? Malay Proverb

Do not attempt to do a thing unless you are sure of yourself, but do not relinquish it simply because someone else is not sure of you.
Stewart E. White

You can succeed if nobody else believes it, but you will never succeed if you don't believe in yourself.
William J. H. Boetchker

In and Out of It All

Jesus said, "It is not what enters into the mouth that defiles the man, but what proceeds out of the mouth, this defiles the man."

Matthew 15:11 NASB

The Story Behind What Jesus Said

In Jesus' day ceremony had become law. A group of leaders took Jesus to task for not insisting that his disciples ceremoniously wash before eating. This was more than just running hands under a faucet. The washing ritual was strict, dictating how the hands were to be immersed, how the washing was to take place, and even the nature of the containers that held the water.

Jesus would have none of it. He taught that people were not defiled by what they ate but by what was within them. Clean hands did not mean a clean heart or a pure conscience. Better to judge people by what came out of their mouths than by what went in.

Hypocrisy is a sharp word. Everyone has met hypocrites and, in honest moments, may even recognize the affliction in themselves. The word means to "play act," to pretend. In *Martin Chuzzlewit*, Charles Dickens described one of his characters as having "affection beaming in one eye, and calculation shining out of the other." Jesus dealt with such people, and so do we.

Genuineness is a rare but noble quality. It was rare in Jesus' day, too. Jesus called for something different. Anyone could act holy, but being holy was another matter. Instead of pretending to be righteous, he called for an honesty that began deep within a person.

Such genuineness is needed today. By changing your inner self, by becoming more than spiritual on the surface, you can change the way you deal with the world, and that will change the way the world deals with you. Whatever you allow to live on the inside will escape to the outside.

One Final Thought

The good you put inside you becomes the glory that others see. Evict the bad, embrace the truth, harbor the beautiful—it will be seen by those around you.

If you think you are better than others, when you really aren't, you are wrong. Galatians 6:3 CEV

If anyone considers himself religious and yet does not keep a tight rein on his tongue, he deceives himself and his religion is worthless.
James 1:26 NIV

Get rid of all malicious behavior and deceit. Don't just pretend to be good! Be done with hypocrisy and jealousy and backstabbing.
1 Peter 2:1 NLT

The wisdom that is from above is first pure, then peaceable, gentle, willing to yield, full of mercy and good fruits, without partiality and without hypocrisy.
James 3:17 NKJV

Do not let loyalty and faithfulness forsake you; bind them around your neck, write them on the tablet of your heart. So you will find favor and good repute in the sight of God and of people.
Proverbs 3:3–4 NRSV

Be humble and gentle. Be patient with each other, making allowance for each other's faults because of your love. Ephesians 4:2 TLB

Hypocrisy in anything whatever may deceive the cleverest and most penetrating man, but the least wide-awake of children recognizes it, and is revolted by it, however ingeniously it may be disguised.

Leo Tolstoy

Neither man nor angel can discern hypocrisy, the only evil that walks invisible, except to God alone.

John Milton

Man who man would be, must rule the empire of himself.

Percy Shelly

Nothing is easier than self-deceit.

Demosthenes

Character is better than ancestry, and personal conduct is more important than the highest parentage.

Thomas Barnardo

Self-command is the main elegance.

Ralph Waldo Emerson

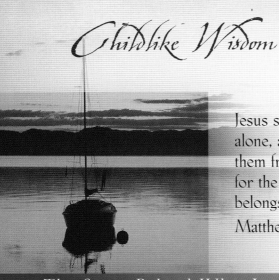

Childlike Wisdom

Jesus said, "Let the children alone, and do not hinder them from coming to Me; for the kingdom of heaven belongs to such as these."

Matthew 19:14 NASB

The Story Behind What Jesus Said

Jesus lived in days where surviving birth and childhood was a great accomplishment. As many as half the children born would die before their twelfth birthday. Anxious parents brought their children to Jesus for a blessing—a natural thing to do. Jesus would lay hands on them, blessing them in the name of the Lord.

The disciples saw this as a waste of the Master's time. In their minds "more important" work waited. So they scolded the parents, trying to send them away. Jesus wasn't in such a hurry that he left people spinning in his wake. He took time to meet their needs, telling the disciples that the kingdom of heaven belonged to innocent children and those like them.

Flying commercial airlines is a good way to get from one place to another quickly, but it is a poor way of taking in scenery. Traveling at six hundred miles per hour at thirty-five thousand feet may get you where you want to be, but it does little to show you where you've been.

Life is filled with pressure. People are pushed and prodded to move from one pressing thing to another. Things get by them, important items get overlooked, lost in the turbulence of their wake—including people. Everything around them changes. Children age, siblings move, and families grow, only to shrink again as children move out on their own.

Those things can never be recaptured; they must be enjoyed at the moment they arrive. Jesus took time out for others, to appreciate them, to bless them. So should you. The past is gone, the future is still around the corner, but you have this moment. Take time to enjoy it.

One Final Thought

Every day moves by in a steady stream of moments. You are the master of those moments, choosing how to spend your time. Look around you. Whom can you bless?

Watch your step. Use your head. Make the most of every chance you get. These are desperate times! Ephesians 5:15–16 THE MESSAGE

Be wise in the way you act with people who are not believers, making the most of every opportunity.
Colossians 4:5 NCV

Let us not become weary in doing good, for at the proper time we will reap a harvest if we do not give up. Therefore, as we have opportunity, let us do good to all people, especially to those who belong to the family of believers.
Galatians 6:9–10 NIV

These things I have told you are all true. I want you to insist on them so that everyone who trusts in God will be careful to do good deeds all the time. These things are good and beneficial for everyone.
Titus 3:8 NLT

See that no one renders evil for evil to anyone, but always pursue what is good both for yourselves and for all.
1 Thessalonians 5:15 NKJV

So teach us to count our days that we may gain a wise heart. Psalm 90:12 NRSV

Jesus loved everyone, but He loved children most of all.
Mother Teresa

The gospel says that the inescapable condition of entrance into the divine fellowship is that we turn and become as a little child.
Elton Trueblood.

Jesus loves me this I know, for the Bible tells me so; little ones to him belong; they are weak, but he is strong.
Anna B. Warner

The stops of a good man are ordered by the Lord as well as his steps.
George Müller

He loves each one of us, as if there were only one of us. Saint Augustine

I love little children, and it is not a slight thing when they who are fresh from God, love us.
Charles Dickens

Jesus, friend of little children, be a friend to me; take my hand and ever keep me, close to thee.
Walter J. Mathams

Everyone Welcome

And hearing this, Jesus said to them, "It is not those who are healthy who need a physician, but those who are sick; I did not come to call the righteous, but sinners."

Mark 2:17 NASB

The Story Behind What Jesus Said

There was headshaking going on. Snickers could be heard. Jesus was eating with the outcasts. What kind of prophet did things like that? Jesus had just called a man to be his disciple. The man was Levi, better known as Matthew.

Matthew was a tax collector. Rome required taxes and appointed locals to gather the money. Matthew was one of those people. Usually tax collectors demanded extra and kept the profit. Jesus not only called Matthew to be a disciple but ate in his home. Matthew had invited his friends—other sinners and tax collectors. That brought a wave of criticism that Jesus used to make a point: There isn't anyone so far removed that Jesus can't love them.

One of life's greatest pressures is fitting in. No one wants to be an outsider, yet most people think they are just that. They first encounter it in school when they learn if they're one of the cool people. Few make it into that group. The rest of the people are left to form relationships with what's left. It was painful then, and it's painful now.

Jesus took a different approach. He welcomed anyone who would follow him without caring if they were inside the acceptable social realm or well outside. Acceptance was open to any who chose it. Unlike cliques encountered today where others decide who is suitable or not, Jesus considers everyone suitable and leaves the choice to join in, in their hands.

Jesus takes you as you are, where you are, when you are. Belonging is easy. His arms are spread wide, and a welcoming smile is on his face. "Come unto me," Jesus said. Many have. Many will.

One Final Thought

Whether popular or outcast, loved or shunned, there is one person waiting for you to join in. His arms are wide, and his heart is open. Take the step.

Because of Christ—dying that death, shedding that blood—you who were once out of it altogether are in on everything.

Ephesians 2:13 THE MESSAGE

Peter began to speak: "I really understand now that to God every person is the same. In every country God accepts anyone who worships him and does what is right."

Acts 10:34–35 NCV

We do not have a High Priest who cannot sympathize with our weaknesses, but was in all points tempted as we are, yet without sin.

Hebrews 4:15 NKJV

He will respond to the prayer of the destitute; he will not despise their plea. Let this be written for a future generation, that a people not yet created may praise the LORD.

Psalm 102:17–18 NIV

This is right and is acceptable in the sight of God our Savior, who desires everyone to be saved and to come to the knowledge of the truth.

1 Timothy 2:3–4 NRSV

Accept each other just as Christ has accepted you; then God will be glorified.

Romans 15:7 NLT

When we are in a situation where Jesus is all we have, we soon discover He is all we really need.
Gigi Graham Tchividjian

Just as I am, thou wilt receive, wilt welcome, pardon, cleanse, relieve:
because thy promise I believe, O Lamb of God, I come.
Charlotte Elliot

Our mind is where our pleasure is, our heart is where our treasure is, our love is where our life is, but all these, our pleasure, treasure, and life, are reposed in Jesus Christ.
Thomas Adams

Jesus hates sin but loves the sinner.
Billy Graham

God's glorious, incomprehensible desire is to meet with humans.
Beth Moore

Not only do we not know God except through Jesus Christ; We do not even know ourselves except through Jesus Christ.
Blaise Pascal

The whole Christ seeks after each sinner, and when the Lord finds it, he gives Himself to that one soul as if He had but that one soul to bless.
C. H. Surgeon

71

Fear and Faith

He said to them, "Why are you afraid? Do you still have no faith?"

Mark 4:40 NASB

The Story Behind What Jesus Said

Jesus' disciples, some trained and experienced fishermen, found themselves in the sharp teeth of a sudden, violent storm. Waves crashed over the bow as the men struggled to row to shore. They were certain that the black waters around them would become their death shroud.

Ironically, Jesus was in the boat, asleep in the stern. In a panic, the disciples woke him to ask if he cared nothing about their imminent doom. Jesus rose and commanded the storm, "Peace, be still!" The gale ceased immediately. However, one more storm was coming, this one from Jesus himself. He asked two pointed questions—a question of fear and a question of faith. The problem was simple: They didn't trust Jesus enough.

Nothing makes a person feel more insignificant than standing in the face of a storm. Wind lashing your hair, rain pelting your skin, and cold air seeping in through your pores all remind you that nature is far more powerful than humans.

There are other types of storms, gales that come not with wind and rain but with fear and dread. Life is uncertain. Family concerns, financial needs, and health problems assail people like a hurricane. Some have trouble weathering such storms. Doubts fill their minds, and they focus their attention on the surging dark waters rather than on Jesus. Such fearful attention replaces faith with fear.

Just as Jesus was in the boat with the disciples when the storm hit, he is also with you when life's gales blow. Do you fix your attention on the storm or upon the one who can still the storm? Jesus still knows how to say, "Peace, be still!"

One Final Thought

Sailing the seas of your life, you encounter frightening storms. But if you take Jesus with you as your constant companion, you can weather anything. Faith replaces fear.

He made the storm stop and the sea be quiet.
Psalm 107:29 CEV

You need not be afraid of disaster or the destruction that comes upon the wicked, for the LORD is your security. He will keep your foot from being caught in a trap.
Proverbs 3:25–26 NLT

When you pass through the waters, I will be with you; and through the rivers, they shall not overflow you. When you walk through the fire, you shall not be burned, nor shall the flame scorch you.
Isaiah 43:2 NKJV

God is our refuge and strength, an ever-present help in trouble. Therefore we will not fear, though the earth give way and the mountains fall into the heart of the sea, though its waters roar and foam and the mountains quake with their surging.
Psalm 46:1–3 NIV

He is close to all who call on him sincerely.
Psalm145:18 TLB

You rule the raging of the sea; when its waves rise, you still them. Psalm 89:9 NRSV

Trust the past to God's mercy, the present to God's love, and the future to God's providence.
Saint Augustine

Stormy weather is what man needs from time to time to remind him he's not really in charge of anything.
Bill Vaughan

I have held many things in my hands, and I have lost them all; but whatever I have placed in God's hands, that I still possess.
Corrie ten Boom

Trials, obstacles, difficulties, and sometimes defeats are the very food of faith.
George Müller

In trouble to be troubled is to have your trouble doubled. Daniel Defoe

Quiet minds that rest in God cannot be perplexed or frightened, but go on in fortune or misfortune at their private pace, like a clock during a thunderstorm.
Robert Louis Stevenson

At the timberline where the storms strike with the most fury, the sturdiest trees are found.
Hudson Taylor

75

Guess What Happened to Me?

Jesus said to him, "Go home to your people and report to them what great things the LORD has done for you, and how He had mercy on you."

Mark 5:19 NASB

The Story Behind What Jesus Said

Six times Jesus cast out demons from individuals. Each time a person under severe bondage was given freedom. The most dramatic case involved a Gentile man who lived among tombs, screaming day and night and wounding himself with sharp stones. When Jesus arrived, the tortured, violent man confronted him.

In a dramatic fashion, Jesus healed the man, and where once stood a fierce lunatic stood a freed person. Word spread, but instead of being impressed, the locals were frightened and implored Jesus to leave. In contrast, the man begged to remain with Jesus. Jesus refused, sending the man home to tell "what great things the Lord has done for you." He went from maniac to missionary in one day.

John Newton was a man with a past. Today he is known for penning the words to "Amazing Grace," a hymn sung around the world. Before he turned his attention to matters of faith he was the cruel captain of a slave-trading ship. He was so vile that his crew hated him, but that didn't keep them from saving his life when he fell overboard in a drunken stupor. In a desperate effort to keep him from drowning, they harpooned him through the leg and drew him back to the ship. He limped for the rest of his life. That limp became a reminder to him that great good can come out of great pain.

On March 10, 1748, Newton's life changed forever. He gave himself to Christ.

Out of that once despicable man came the sweet words of "Amazing Grace." He was changed, and, like the demon-possessed man Jesus liberated, Newton went back to his family and friends and told of the wonderful things the Lord had done for him.

One Final Thought

God has done many wonderful things for you, and like the demon-possessed man, you need to tell others. Speaking of God's faithfulness and your faith in Christ is liberating in a thousand ways. Whom can you tell?

He has not ignored the suffering of the needy. He has not turned and walked away. He has listened to their cries for help. Psalm 22:24 NLT

All who worship God, come here and listen; I will tell you everything God has done for me.
Psalm 66:16 CEV

It is my pleasure to tell you about the miraculous signs and wonders that the Most High God has performed for me. How great are his signs, how mighty his wonders! His kingdom is an eternal kingdom; his dominion endures from generation to generation.
Daniel 4:2–3 NIV

I have not hidden Your righteousness within my heart; I have declared Your faithfulness and Your salvation; I have not concealed Your lovingkindness and Your truth from the great assembly.
Psalm 40:10 NKJV

Always give thanks for everything to our God and Father in the name of our LORD Jesus Christ.
Ephesians 5:20 TLB

Through Jesus, therefore, let us continually offer to God a sacrifice of praise—the fruit of lips that confess his name. Hebrews 13:15 NIV

When I saw the unwearied patience, that unflagging zeal, those enlightened sons of Africa, I became a Christian at his side, though he never spoke to me about it.

Henry Morton Stanley
(about missionary David
Livingstone)

Remember, a small light will do a great deal when it is in a very dark place. Put one little tallow candle in the middle of a large hall, and it will give a good deal of light.

D. L. Moody

If a man cannot be a Christian in the place where he is, he cannot be a Christian anywhere.

Henry Ward Beecher

Preach the gospel every day; if necessary use words. Saint Francis of Assisi

Praising God is one of the highest and purest acts of religion. In prayer we act like men; in praise we act like angels.

Thomas Watson

If any one would tell you the shortest, surest way to all happiness and all perfection, he must tell you to make it a rule to yourself to thank and praise God for everything that happens to you.

William Law

Permission to Leave

> He said to them, "Come
> away by yourselves to
> a secluded place and rest
> a while."
>
> Mark 6:31 NASB

The Story Behind What Jesus Said

Twelve disciples stood under the warm Galilean sun and
listened to Jesus as he assigned them their task. They were
to go out in pairs to work miracles and preach.
Frightening stuff. It's one thing to follow a bold and
respected teacher like Jesus; it's quite another to go out in
his name and preach to strangers. They went and had
enormous success.

Their success came with a demanding price. While all
went well, they were tired, worn, and hungry. The crowds
continued to follow, pressing close in suffocating numbers. Jesus knew their need and gave a command—not a
suggestion—to move to a secluded place and rest. They
needed it; Jesus insisted upon it.

IN HIS OWN WORDS

In this workaholic world it has become difficult to justify rest. Corporations offer family benefits but demand such long hours from executives and workers that children see too little of their parents and spouses struggle to stay connected. Too many see rest as unproductive and hard to justify.

Resting is part of God's personal plan for you. Humans were designed to work, but they were also designed to relax. Work without rest is an unbalanced equation and damaging to all concerned. Jesus took frequent rests (ten are mentioned in the New Testament), often moving into outlying regions and up mountainsides to get time alone. If Jesus needed rest, then it is certain you need rest.

Hard as it is for many to believe, resting is a godly pursuit. Jesus insisted that his disciples have time off. He insists that you take time off. Reflect. Recline. Refresh. Recharge. Recreate. It's a godly thing to do. It is how you've been designed.

One Final Thought

Take time to take time. You deserve an opportunity to take a breath and become reacquainted with yourself and with life. God has given you permission to relax for a while.

By the seventh day God had finished his work. On the seventh day he rested from all his work. Genesis 2:2 THE MESSAGE

Then I will be able to come to you with a happy heart by the will of God, and we can refresh each other. Romans 15:32 TLB

There is a special rest still waiting for the people of God. For all who enter into God's rest will find rest from their labors, just as God rested after creating the world. Hebrews 4:9–10 NLT

Unless the LORD builds the house, its builders labor in vain. Unless the LORD watches over the city, the watchmen stand guard in vain. In vain you rise early and stay up late, toiling for food to eat— for he grants sleep to those he loves. Psalm 127:1–2 NIV

I will give rest and strength to those who are weak and tired. Jeremiah 31:25 NCV

The sleep of a laboring man is sweet, whether he eats little or much. Ecclesiastes 5:12 NKJV

It is the part of a Christian to take care of his own body for the very purpose that by its soundness and well-being he may be enabled to labor for the aid of those who are in want, that thus the stronger member may serve the weaker member.
Martin Luther

*Each morning sees some
    task begin,
Each evening sees it close;
Something attempted,
    something done,
Has earned a night's repose.*
Henry Wadsworth Longfellow

Oh Lord! Thou knowest how busy I must be this day: If I forget thee, do not thou forget me.
Sir Jacob Astley

If a man is cruel to himself, how can we expect him to be compassionate to others? Jewish Proverb

Christ is not only a remedy for your weariness and trouble, but He will give you an abundance of the contrary, joy and delight.
Jonathan Edwards

Work is not always required of a man. There is such a thing as sacred idleness, the cultivation of which is now fearfully neglected.
George MacDonald

Impossible Possibilities

> Jesus said to him, "'If You can?' All things are possible to him who believes."
>
> Mark 9:23 NASB

The Story Behind What Jesus Said

A man approached Jesus' disciples with a plea to help his possessed son. What agony it must have been to helplessly watch his boy cast to the ground, convulsing, unable to do anything. The disciples were powerless.

Jesus arrived in time to hear their discussion. As if on cue, the boy began to convulse violently, falling to the ground. Terrified, the father begged, "If You can do anything, help us!" His words were dripping with doubt. Why not? He had been disappointed so many times. But here is the difference. He was not speaking to an ordinary person but to Jesus, who can make ordinary extraordinary. "All things are possible to him who believes." A moment later, the boy was healed.

Nothing brings doubt as fast as despair. Life is not easy; often it is not fair. Eighty-three million people seek help from alternative medicine every year, spending nearly thirty million dollars annually. Many do so out of desperation. Everyone and everything else has failed them. It's hard to be critical.

Belief is a powerful force. It has the potential to change your thinking, your behavior, and your emotions and to give you hope. Lack of belief can do the opposite. Belief empowers you to trust, frees you to act, and releases you from suffocating worry.

Hard times come to everyone; to some more than others. Belief in God's goodness and Christ's love gets you through those ebony nights of anguish. Your help may not come in the form of a miracle. It may come in loving support of a family member, the strong hands of a friend, or in the courage to face with dignity whatever comes your way. Belief always helps.

One Final Thought

The father cried out, "I do believe; help my unbelief." It's a powerful and liberating prayer, one every Christian should pray. Today is a good time to start.

Let all who run to you for protection always sing joyful songs. Provide shelter for those who truly love you and let them rejoice. Psalm 5:11 CEV

Trust in the LORD with all your heart; do not depend on your own understanding. Seek his will in all you do, and he will direct your paths. . . . Don't lose sight of good planning and insight. Hang on to them, for they fill you with life and bring you honor and respect.
Proverbs 3:5–6, 21–22 NLT

Blessed is the man who trusts in the LORD, and whose hope is the LORD.
Jeremiah 17:7 NKJV

You will keep in perfect peace all who trust in you, whose thoughts are fixed on you! Trust in the LORD always, for the LORD GOD is the eternal Rock.
Isaiah 26:3–4 NLT

Ask boldly, believingly, without a second thought. People who "worry their prayers" are like wind-whipped waves.
James 1:6 THE MESSAGE

The LORD is good, a stronghold in a day of trouble; he protects those who take refuge in him. Nahum 1:7 NRSV

He does not believe that does not live according to his belief.
Thomas Fuller

I can get more out of God by believing Him for one minute than by shouting at Him all night.
Smith Wigglesworth

For I seek not to understand in order that I may believe; but I believe in order that I may understand, for I believe for this reason: that unless I believe, I cannot understand.
Saint Anselm of Canterbury

A man's real belief is that which he lives by. What a man believes is the thing he does, not the thing he thinks.
George MacDonald

As the body lives by breathing, so the soul lives by believing. Thomas Brooks

There is no other method of living piously and justly, than that of depending upon God.
John Calvin

All I have seen teaches me to trust the Creator for all I have not seen.
Ralph Waldo Emerson

Making It Look Easy

Jesus looked at them and said, "There are some things that people cannot do, but God can do anything."

Mark 10:27 CEV

The Story Behind What Jesus Said

A man ran to Jesus and then abruptly knelt. His clothing made it clear that he was rich beyond the average person's dreams. One thing his wealth couldn't buy was assurance of the future. He had kept all the commandments but still felt that something was missing. The question burning in his heart came out: "What shall I do to inherit eternal life?"

The answer was shocking. Jesus said to sell everything he owned and join the disciples. He left grieving. A heartbroken Jesus watched him go. The disciples were as surprised as the man. When told by Jesus that it was difficult for the wealthy to enter the Kingdom of God, they wondered, "How then can the rest of us enter?"

With Jesus there is always more than meets the eye—or ear. His statements were layered with more truth than expected. In Jesus' day being rich was a sign of God's blessing. When the disciples heard that it was difficult for the wealthy to enter the Kingdom of God, they assumed it was impossible for poor people like themselves.

Jesus' message to them is the same message to you: "With God, all things are possible." Life is a difficult walk, but you needn't make it alone. You may feel that there has been too much wrong done in your life for God to open his arms to you, that the future is made dark by the past. Despite appearances, God can deal with the matter.

The good news is that nothing is beyond the notice, the concern, and the power of God. In such situations depend on the power of the one who is not intimidated by the impossible.

One Final Thought

God specializes in the impossible, and he specializes in you. It only takes a little movement to shift your eyes from the problem to God, your solution.

Keep up your courage, men, for I have faith in God that it will happen just as he told me.

Acts 27:25 NIV

The LORD said to Moses, "Is there any limit to my power? Now you will see whether or not my word comes true!"

Numbers 11:23 NLT

O LORD God! You have made the heavens and earth by your great power; nothing is too hard for you!

Jeremiah 32:17 TLB

"You didn't have enough faith," Jesus told them. "I assure you, even if you had faith as small as a mustard seed you could say to this mountain, 'Move from here to there,' and it would move. Nothing would be impossible."

Matthew 17:20 NLT

God can do anything, you know—far more than you could ever imagine or guess or request in your wildest dreams! He does it not by pushing us around but by working within us, his Spirit deeply and gently within us.

Ephesians 3:20 THE MESSAGE

For with God nothing will be impossible.

Luke 1:37 NKJV

*Faith sees the invisible,
believes the unbelievable,
and receives the impossible.*
Corrie ten Boom

*Don't think so much about
who is for or against you,
rather give all your care
that God be with you in
everything you do.*
Thomas à Kempis

*God is not a deceiver, that
he should offer to support
us, and then, when we
lean upon Him, should
slip away from us.*
Saint Augustine

*I have learned to use the
word "impossible" with
the greatest caution.*
Werner Von Braun

*We have a God who delights
in the impossibilities.* Andrew Murray

*This is the creator:
by his love, our Father;
by his power, our Lord;
by his wisdom, our
maker and designer.*
Irenaeus

*Until we reach for the
impossible through fer-
vent, faith-filled prayer,
we will never fulfill our
created purpose!*
David Smithers

The Two Directions of Love

Jesus replied, "The most important one is this . . . 'Love the LORD your God with all your heart.' . . . The second most important commandment is this: 'Love your neighbor as you love yourself.'"

Mark 12:29–31 GNT

The Story Behind What Jesus Said

It was a point-blank question that garnered a point-blank answer. In a world where hundreds of regulations governed daily life, the natural concern was, "Which is the most important rule?" It was a scribe who asked the question, a man whose job was to copy and recopy Scripture. Such repetition made him an expert in such matters. He tested Jesus' expertise—and wasn't disappointed.

The first and foremost command centered on how a person related to God—one's vertical connection. The relationship with God came from love, a love that involved the whole person. But Jesus added another command, a horizontal connection. Loving God was not complete unless one loved his neighbor to the same degree he loved himself.

A bicycle wheel is a remarkable piece of engineering: a single hub connected to a rim by spokes. The rim is useless without the hub; the hub cannot function without the rim. Connecting it all together are spokes. You are the hub and are connected to God and those around you by an infinite number of spokes. What you do with those connections makes a difference in the kind of life you live.

Your love of God involves every part of you: Your emotions (heart), your being (soul), your thoughts (mind), and your efforts (strength). Such love is a choice.

You have no control over what others think of you, but you have absolute control over what you think of others. Love is the key, and that love is not based on the worthiness of your neighbors. You can choose to love them as you love yourself. It's not easy, but it is necessary for their good and for yours.

One Final Thought

What you think of God determines what you think of people; what you think of others governs what you think of God—and that determines what you think of yourself.

The Two Directions of Love

Love never hurts a neighbor, so loving is obeying all the law. Romans 13:10 NCV

He has showed you, O man, what is good. And what does the LORD require of you? To act justly and to love mercy and to walk humbly with your God.

Micah 6:8 NIV

Dear children, let us stop just saying we love each other; let us really show it by our actions. It is by our actions that we know we are living in the truth, so we will be confident when we stand before the LORD.

1 John 3:18–19 NLT

Write these commandments that I've given you today on your hearts. Get them inside of you and then get them inside your children.

Deuteronomy 6:6
THE MESSAGE

Owe no one anything except to love one another, for he who loves another has fulfilled the law.

Romans 13:8 NKJV

God himself has said that one must love not only God, but his brother too. 1 John 4:21 TLB

Charity begins at home, and justice begins next door.
Charles Dickens

I am to become a Christ to my neighbor and be for him what Christ is for me.
Martin Luther

The love of God is the first and great commandment. But love of our neighbor is the means by which we obey it.
Saint Augustine

The love of our neighbor is the only door out of the dungeon of self.
George MacDonald

Those who do not love their neighbor abhor God. Saint John of the Cross

No man is an island, entire of itself; every man is a piece of the continent, a part of the main; any man's death diminishes me, because I am involved in mankind; and therefore never send to know for whom the bell tolls; it tolls for thee.
John Donne

The Doer and the Critic

Jesus said, "Let her alone; why do you bother her? She has done a good deed to Me."

Mark 14:6 NASB

The Story Behind What Jesus Said

How do you honor Jesus? One woman chose a unique demonstration of love. Mary, the sister of Martha and Lazarus, joined Jesus at a gathering in the home of Simon the leper. Mary didn't go to the gathering empty-handed; she took a small, alabaster jar of perfume, a pint of liquid processed from a plant found in India. It cost the equivalent of one year's wages. She broke the container's long neck and poured the substance on Jesus' head.

It was common to anoint the heads of kings and important others, but not with such an expensive substance. Mary felt compelled to give her very best—and she was harshly criticized for it. Jesus took her side.

Abraham Lincoln—whom people now view as a hero—once said, "If I tried to read, much less answer, all the criticisms made of me, and all the attacks leveled against me, this office would have to be closed for all other business." Greatness, wisdom, achievement, and even righteousness cannot exempt anyone from criticism. It doesn't take long to learn that critics are everywhere.

Sometimes a little criticism is deserved; many times it is unfair. When, like Mary, you are the target of harsh words, the tendency is to stop doing the good and to surrender to the negative opinions of others. Mary continued to do what she felt led to do. So should you.

No one builds monuments to critics. Bold and brave and determined people are another matter. They go on to be examples of courage and truth. Do a good thing in the name of Jesus, and don't listen to those who stand in the shadows and complain.

One Final Thought

The hiss of the critics will be forever in the ears of those who choose to do right, and that should make no difference at all. Do the good.

In God I have put my trust; I will not be afraid.
What can man do to me? Psalm 56:11 NKJV

Blessed are you when people insult you, persecute you, lie, and say all kinds of evil things about you because of me.
Matthew 5:11 GOD'S WORD

Hear me, you who know what is right, you people who have my law in your hearts: Do not fear the reproach of men or be terrified by their insults.
Isaiah 51:7 NIV

Count it a blessing when you suffer for being a Christian. This shows that God's glorious Spirit is with you.
1 Peter 4:14 CEV

Yet what we suffer now is nothing compared to the glory he will give us later.
Romans 8:18 TLB

The LORD despises the way of the wicked, but he loves those who pursue godliness.

Proverbs 15:9 NLT

*Criticism is easy;
achievement is
more difficult.*
Winston Churchill

*Humble yourself,
and cease to care
what men think.*
A. W. Tozer

*How much easier it is to be
critical than to be correct.*
Benjamin Disraeli

*It is much easier to fix
blame than fix problems.*
Kathleen Parker

*Any fool can criticize, condemn,
and complain—and most do.*
Benjamin Franklin

*If it is painful for you to
criticize your friends,
you're safe in doing it; if
you take the slightest pleasure in it, that's the time to
hold your tongue.*
Alice Duer Miller

*Criticism comes easier than
craftsmanship.*
Zeuxis of Athens

Two Is a Big Number

> Jesus said, "For where two or three have gathered together in My name, I am there in their midst."
>
> Matthew 18:20 NASB

The Story Behind What Jesus Said

How small can a congregation get before a church ceases to be a church? Pretty small. To the Jews of Jesus' day, ten men were required to form a synagogue. Many, however, believed that God could be experienced in a much smaller group. Jesus made that very point.

Ancient Jewish law required that there be at least two witnesses to a crime before judgment could be brought to bear upon the accused. But people witness more than crimes; they also witness good and beautiful things, such as worship. By building on this principle, Jesus made sure that his followers knew that he was with them even if there were only two present to worship. They were witnesses to faith.

There is power in groups. Large numbers of people make a dynamic force. There is power in the few as well, even in the one. A one-time popular poster read: "Me and God make a majority." There's truth in that statement. God is in the multitudes, but he is also in the midst of the two.

Jesus made a promise, and it was far more than poetic speech. He promised his presence to any number of people who gathered in his name. From two to twenty thousand, Jesus has it covered. There is no place where Jesus can't join you, no time when you can't find him.

It's desire that makes the difference, a hunger for fellowship. Many people know what it is like for Jesus to join them where they are. Church happens with or without walls; worship is sent heavenward with many voices or just one. It might seem like new math, but it is a powerful and liberating truth.

One Final Thought

Look around you. Jesus is before you, behind you, next to you, above you. There is great comfort in that and greater opportunity for divine, life-changing fellowship.

May the grace of our LORD Jesus Christ, the love of God, and the fellowship of the Holy Spirit be with you all. 2 Corinthians 13:13 NLT

Haggai gave the LORD's message to the people: "I will be with you—that is my promise."
Haggai 1:13 GNT

At the name of Jesus every knee shall bow in heaven and on earth and under the earth, and every tongue shall confess that Jesus Christ is Lord, to the glory of God the Father.
Philippians 2:10–11 TLB

Go and make disciples of all nations, baptizing them in the name of the Father and of the Son and of the Holy Spirit. . . . And surely I am with you always, to the very end of the age.
Matthew 28:19–20 NIV

Everyone who confesses that Jesus is God's Son participates continuously in an intimate relationship with God.
1 John 4:15 THE MESSAGE

At that day you will know that I am in My Father, and you in Me, and I in you.
John 14:20 NKJV

Christ is my Savior. He is my life. He is everything to me in heaven and earth.

Sadhu Sundar Singh

The presence of Jesus Christ in our lives is the most beautiful thing that can happen to us, for then we are never alone again!

Joan Winmill Brown

Many are willing that Christ should be something, but few will consent that Christ should be everything.

Alexander Moody Stuart

He became what we are that he might make us what he is.

Saint Athanasius of Alexandria

Christ is a substitute for everything, but nothing is a substitute for Christ.

H. A. Ironside

Christ be with me, Christ before me, Christ behind me, Christ in me, Christ beneath me, Christ above me, Christ on my right, Christ on my left, Christ when I lie down, Christ when I sit down, Christ when I arise.

Saint Patrick

Propelled by Purpose

He said to them, "I must preach the kingdom of God to the other cities also, for I was sent for this purpose."

Luke 4:43 NASB

The Story Behind What Jesus Said

Jesus had left the lakeside town of Capernaum, where he had been received with enthusiasm. Crowds followed him, pressing in to hear, to see, and to touch the great teacher. The healings worked by Jesus had brought great crowds, so much so that peace could only be found by retreating to a secluded area.

There must have been a temptation to leave it all behind. So many demands, so many needs, so many hurts and troubles; it's a wonder that Jesus didn't quit early on. But Jesus was driven by a purpose. Others needed to hear his words, listen to his teaching, and embrace his truth. Weary or not, Jesus was determined to go to the other cities and preach.

Businesses have mission statements that define why they exist and what it is they do. Some are short and allow for change; others are long and detailed. The most successful businesses clearly understand their purpose. Ford Motor Company has stated this as their vision: "To become the world's leading consumer company for automotive products and services." Simple and to the point.

People should have purpose. You should have purpose. From the beginning, Jesus knew exactly what he had come to do. Your purpose may be rooted in your family or your art or your goals. Microsoft's motto is "Your potential, our passion." What is your passion? What moves you forward even in times of difficulty?

Jesus moved on with his work to "seek and save that which is lost" (Luke 19:10). Jesus' purpose was centered on the needs of others and that has changed millions of lives. Your highest purpose is measured by the benefit others receive from your existence.

One Final Thought

Whether invisibly or publicly, your existence makes a difference in the lives of others. Have a driving purpose that moves you, motivates you, sustains you—then live it.

I say to the rest of you, dear brothers and sisters, never get tired of doing good.

2 Thessalonians 3:13 NLT

Speak encouraging words to one another. Build up hope so you'll all be together in this.

1 Thessalonians 5:11 THE MESSAGE

We have many parts in the one body, and all these parts have different functions. In the same way, though we are many, we are one body in union with Christ, and we are all joined to each other as different parts of one body.

Romans 12:4–5 GNT

Make it your ambition to lead a quiet life, to mind your own business and to work with your hands, just as we told you, so that your daily life may win the respect of outsiders and so that you will not be dependent on anybody.

1 Thessalonians 4:11–12 NIV

Whatever you do, do it heartily, as to the Lord and not to men.

Colossians 3:23 NKJV

Here is my final conclusion: fear God and obey his commandments, for this is the entire duty of man. Ecclesiastes 12:13 TLB

All labor that uplifts humanity has dignity and importance and should be undertaken with painstaking excellence.
Martin Luther King Jr.

I long to accomplish a great and noble task; but it is my chief duty to accomplish small tasks as if they were great and noble.
Helen Keller

Great minds have purposes, others have wishes.
Washington Irving

Action springs not from thought, but from a readiness for responsibility.
Dietrich Bonhoeffer

The chief end of man is to glorify God and enjoy Him forever.
Catechism of 1646

If your father and mother, your sister and brother, if the very cat and dog in the house, are not happier for your being Christian, it is a question whether you really are.
Hudson Taylor

A Different Way of Doing Things

When He had finished speaking, He said to Simon, "Put out into the deep water and let down your nets for a catch."

Luke 5:4 NASB

The Story Behind What Jesus Said

Most of the disciples were fishermen; those who weren't were familiar with the trade. Peter was an expert. Fishing had been his life and that of his family. He and others had fished all night but had come up empty. Frustration was made worse by embarrassment.

That morning Jesus stepped into Peter's boat to better be able to speak to the gathering crowds. Then came the command to push out into deep water. It made no sense to Peter, who protested that the time was wrong, the place was wrong, and he had already done his best. Still, Peter did as he was told. The end result? More fish than the boat could hold. Jesus' ways are often different and surprising.

Great lessons come by way of surprise. Just when you think you have the world figured out, something happens to change your mind. In this technological age people have come to think that all things can be reduced to computer binary code, a series of ones and zeros perfectly laid out. Their instincts tell them otherwise.

Your world may operate today as it did yesterday and the day before. That's the way it should be. When Jesus intervenes, things operate differently. A question may percolate up in your heart, a suggestion to do something different, to be bold. When you sense that suggestion is from God and follow it, it's called faith—faith that Jesus is not confined to the rules that govern your life. He is still King of Kings.

It takes courage to push out into the deep water where reason tells you nothing waits. But when Jesus is in your boat, anything can happen. Trust in him.

One Final Thought

The daily routine can be useful, but there are times to row out into the deep water, row where Jesus tells you, fish where he says, and get ready for the unexpected.

The people said unto Joshua, The LORD our God will we serve, and his voice will we obey.

Joshua 24:24 KJV

My own hand laid the foundations of the earth, and my right hand spread out the heavens; when I summon them, they all stand up together.

Isaiah 48:13 NIV

I am the LORD, the God of all the peoples of the world. Is anything too hard for me?

Jeremiah 32:27 NLT

O Lord GOD, You have begun to show Your servant Your greatness and Your mighty hand, for what god is there in heaven or on earth who can do anything like Your works and Your mighty deeds?

Deuteronomy 3:24 NKJV

Your hand controls power and might, and it is at your discretion that men are made great and given strength.

1 Chronicles 29:12 TLB

You, LORD God, have done many wonderful things, and you have planned marvelous things for us. No one is like you! I would never be able to tell all you have done. Psalm 40:5 CEV

It is morally impossible to exercise trust in God while there is failure to wait upon Him for guidance and direction.

D. E. Hoste

I am satisfied that when the Almighty wants me to do or not to do any particular thing, he finds a way of letting me know.

Abraham Lincoln

How often it occurs to me, as it must to you, that it is far easier simply to cooperate with God!

Beth Moore

Never be afraid to trust an unknown future to a known God.

Corrie ten Boom

We are His glory when we follow His ways. Florence Nightingale

Our duty is to see whether God is with us; whether we expect great things from Him; whether we do not practically place Him far off, forgetting that, if He is, He is about us, speaking to us words that have not been heard before, guiding us to paths on which earlier generations have not been able to enter.

Brooke Foss Westcott

Treating an Enemy?

Jesus said, "Bless those who curse you, pray for those who mistreat you. Whoever hits you on the cheek, offer him the other also."

Luke 6:28–29 NASB

The Story Behind What Jesus Said

It's easier to hate than to love, easier to plan revenge than to forgive. Jesus taught many things that went against the norm, the accepted practice of the time. People of Jesus' day were familiar with heated curses thrown against an antagonist or enemy. It was a natural and human thing to do, but Jesus taught a different response.

When cursed, he taught that a blessing should be the chosen answer. Prayer and giving were to be the reply to mistreatment. How odd this must have sounded. "He's telling us to do the opposite of what we have always done," people might have protested. That was the point. Returning anger for anger, hatred for hatred solves nothing. Love, however, solves everything.

Control is a powerful thing—especially self-control. Hydroplaning is something that every driver experiences. The tires of the car break traction on a wet road and the vehicle begins to slide. It's an odd and often dangerous situation. One moment you're in control of two thousand pounds of vehicle, and the next moment the car seems to have a mind of its own.

Emotions can skid out of control when confronted by harsh words, ill treatment, or insult. The knee-jerk response is to return the insults, hatred, anger, or offense. Jesus teaches you should do otherwise, that you should maintain control and choose your response. It's a matter of control. When someone insults you and you give back as good as you get, then the offender is in control. When you choose to bless and not curse, you are in control. Thoughtless response is surrender to the situation; controlled reaction is victory. To deal with evil, deliver a response of love.

One Final Thought

Self-control does more good, brings more satisfaction, and creates the greatest likelihood of change in the life of the offender and the offended. Give better than you receive.

Don't be glad when your enemies meet disaster, and don't rejoice when they stumble.

Proverbs 24:17 GNT

Everyone must live in harmony, be sympathetic, love each other, have compassion, and be humble.

1 Peter 3:8 GOD'S WORD

Stop being mean, bad-tempered and angry. Quarreling, harsh words, and dislike of others should have no place in your lives. Instead, be kind to each other, tender-hearted, forgiving one another, just as God has forgiven you because you belong to Christ.

Ephesians 4:31–32 TLB

He did not retaliate when he was insulted. When he suffered, he did not threaten to get even. He left his case in the hands of God, who always judges fairly.

1 Peter 2:23 NLT

Never pay back evil for evil to anyone. Do things in such a way that everyone can see you are honorable. Do your part to live in peace with everyone, as much as possible.

Romans 12:17–18 NLT

If your enemy is hungry, give him food to eat; if he is thirsty, give him water to drink. Proverbs 25:21 NIV

*He who reigns within him-
self, and rules passions,
desires and fears, is more
than a king.*
John Milton

*In Jesus and for Him, ene-
mies and friends alike are to
be loved.*
Thomas à Kempis

*If you want to make
peace with your enemy,
you have to work with
your enemy. Then he
becomes your partner.*
Nelson Mandela

*It's not the mountain we
conquer but ourselves.*
Sir Edmund Hillary

The best way to destroy an enemy is to make him a friend. Abraham Lincoln

*That you [pray for your
enemy] willingly, that you
are glad to do it, that you
are delighted according to
the inner man to obey
your Lord and pray for
your enemy—this shows
that you are gold.*
Saint Augustine

*A man that studieth
revenge keeps his own
wounds green.*
Francis Bacon

Gaining by Giving

Jesus said, "They will pour into your lap a good measure—pressed down, shaken together, and running over. For by your standard of measure it will be measured to you in return."

Luke 6:38 NASB

The Story Behind What Jesus Said

If you could stand in the marketplace of ancient Israel, you'd see a bustle of activity. People buying, selling, and arguing over prices. You'd also see someone buying grain. It was the custom to pour grain from the seller's container into the purchaser's container. In an act of generosity, the merchant would fill his measure so full that grain would rain down from it. The buyer would hold out the front part of her loose outer garment to form a pouch and receive more than she requested. It was called a good measure.

It was good for the buyer and created a good reputation for the merchant. Jesus used this everyday example to send home the point that the best way to get is to give and give generously.

"It takes money to make money" is an old saying and an accurate one. The well-worn business maxim teaches that something must be given in order for something to be returned. Ancient merchants were dependent upon their reputations. Generous owners could expect lines to grow outside their market; miserly ones could only watch people defect to competitors.

Giving of yourself and of your means brings returns; giving extra brings great returns. God knows the hearts of all people and rewards those who find pleasure in sharing some of their best. This goes beyond your money and includes time, kindness, and even expertise.

You should not give just to get, but by giving you will see blessings come in unexpected ways, and not just in the thanks of men and women, but in the tangible appreciation of God. When you give of yourself you invest in others and in your spiritual wealth. God practices what he preaches—he knows how to give.

One Final Thought

From the bank of your heart and mind, give to others what you can, when you can. You will see that you can't outgive the Creator. Give until it feels good.

Timeless Wisdom for Everyday Living

You shall generously give to him, and your heart shall not be grieved when you give to him, because for this thing the LORD your God will bless you in all your work and in all your undertakings. Deuteronomy 15:10 NASB

Honor the LORD with your wealth, with the first-fruits of all your crops; then your barns will be filled to overflowing.
Proverbs 3:9–10a NIV

"Bring to the storehouse a full tenth of what you earn so there will be food in my house. Test me in this," says the LORD All-Powerful. "I will open the windows of heaven for you and pour out all the blessings you need."
Malachi 3:10 NCV

Everyone must make up his own mind as to how much he should give. Don't force anyone to give more than he really wants to, for cheerful givers are the ones God prizes.
2 Corinthians 9:7 TLB

Right now you have plenty and can help them. Then at some other time they can share with you when you need it.
2 Corinthians 8:14 NLT

He who has pity on the poor lends to the LORD, and He will pay back what he has given.
Proverbs 19:17 NKJV

A man there was, though some did count him mad, the more he cast away the more he had.
John Bunyan

If there be any truer measure of man than by what he does, it must be by what he gives.
Robert South

We make a living by what we get, but we make a life by what we give.
Norman MacEwan

The world says, "The more you take, the more you have." Christ says, "The more you give, the more you are."
Frederick Buechner

Blessed are those who can give without remembering and take without forgetting. Elizabeth Bibesco

Those who bring sunshine to the lives of others cannot keep it from themselves.
Sir James M. Barrie

Unless we give part of ourselves away, unless we can live with other people and understand them and help them, we are missing the most essential part of our own lives.
Harold Taylor

119

Unexpected Faith

Jesus was surprised when he heard this; he turned around and said to the crowd following him, "I tell you, I have never found faith like this, not even in Israel."

Luke 7:9 GNT

The Story Behind What Jesus Said

No two people were more different. Jesus was an itinerate preacher, poor and without social position—a carpenter with miracles in his hands. The centurion was a Roman army officer who oversaw the work and training of one hundred soldiers. He was one of the Roman conquerors who held Israel in their tight fists.

This centurion was different. Beneath the breastplate of his armor beat the heart of a man who respected the Jews, built a synagogue for them, and cared for his servants, including one who lay sick and dying. Despite his high social rank, he was too humble to approach Jesus to ask for help. He sent others in his place. Jesus saw this as great and unexpected faith.

Someone said, "Faith is not believing that God can, but that God will!" The centurion ran the risk of ridicule from his peers and rejection by Jesus but sent for Christ's help anyway. That's how strong his love for his servant was; that's how great his faith in Christ was.

One of the great hymns is "Trust and Obey" by John Sammis. As the song was being sung in a church, a child—as children sometimes do—misheard the title and sang the chorus incorrectly as "trust and okay." Maybe he wasn't so far off.

Faith is the application of belief to life. It is not an academic principle; it's a tool for daily living. Like the centurion, you need to trust Christ with your problems and with your life—even if it seems to everyone else an unexpected and unlikely thing for you to do. Whether you're an outsider or an insider, Jesus is the one to turn to. Trust and okay.

One Final Thought

Jesus saw a powerful man's request for help as a mighty display of faith. Nothing has changed. The most courageous thing you can do is approach Jesus in faith and belief.

Faith comes from hearing, and hearing by the word of Christ. Romans 10:17 NASB

This is what God says we must do: Believe on the name of his Son Jesus Christ, and love one another.
1 John 3:23 TLB

Faith is the substance of things hoped for, the evidence of things not seen. By faith we understand that the worlds were framed by the word of God, so that the things which are seen were not made of things which are visible.
Hebrews 11:1, 3 NKJV

In the gospel a righteousness from God is revealed, a righteousness that is by faith from first to last, just as it is written: "The righteous will live by faith."
Romans 1:17 NIV

May God give you peace, dear brothers and sisters, and love with faith, from God the Father and the LORD Jesus Christ.
Ephesians 6:23 NLT

We walk by faith, not by sight. 2 Corinthians 5:7 KJV

Faith is like radar that sees through the fog—the reality of things at a distance that the human eye cannot see.
Corrie ten Boom

Fear imprisons, faith liberates; fear paralyzes, faith empowers; fear disheartens, faith encourages; fear sickens, faith heals; fear makes useless, faith make serviceable.
Harry Emerson Fosdick

Trust and obey,
for there's no other way
To be happy in Jesus,
but to trust and obey.
John H. Sammis

Faith is an act of a finite being who is grasped by, and turned to, the infinite.
Paul Tillich

Faith is a sounder guide than reason. Reason can go only so far, but faith has no limits. Blaise Pascal

Let this be well weighed and considered, that the justified person lives and performs every act of spiritual life by faith. Everything is promised to, and is received by, faith.
William Romaine

Faith is to prayer what the feather is to the arrow; without faith it will not hit the mark.
J. C. Ryle

123

The Fruit of Forgiveness

Jesus said, "For this reason I say to you, her sins, which are many, have been forgiven, for she loved much; but he who is forgiven little, loves little."

Luke 7:47 NASB

The Story Behind What Jesus Said

Jesus was invited to the home of a religious leader named Simon. In the spacious house, Jesus reclined at the dinner table. Unlike today, people did not sit at the table, but reclined on benches, their feet extended behind them. Neighbors joined the gathering. One neighbor made her way to the table.

She was considered a "sinner" and was most likely a prostitute. Moved by love, the woman wet Jesus' feet with her tears, wiped them clean with her hair, and anointed his feet with an expensive perfume. Simon could only find fault with the woman and with Jesus for allowing the display. Jesus recognized the woman's repentance and Simon's hard heart. She loved much because she was forgiven much.

Stories do more than entertain; they inform. In this event Jesus told a parable—an earthly story with a heavenly meaning—to teach a life-changing truth. There were two men, each in debt. One man owed a modest amount of money; the other owed a great deal more. The lender forgave their debts. Jesus then asked, "Simon, which of the two will love the lender more?" Simon got it right: "The one who owed much."

Unforgiven sin is a prison; forgiveness is freedom. Still, some people avoid the topic as if they have become too attached to the sin or too proud to admit that they need forgiveness. Forgiveness always produces the fruit of joy. Much forgiveness leads to great happiness. That joy is waiting for you, no matter what needs to be forgiven. No one is beyond forgiveness.

You can't erase the past, but you can release its hold on you. That's the power of confession and forgiveness.

One Final Thought

Push through whatever crowd stands between you and forgiveness, and let Jesus take the pressing weight of sin from your shoulders. You'll find that Jesus is very approachable.

If we confess our sins, he is faithful and just to forgive us our sins, and to cleanse us from all unrighteousness. 1 John 1:9 KJV

God is not unjust; he will not forget your work and the love you have shown him as you have helped his people and continue to help them.
Hebrews 6:10 NIV

A man who refuses to admit his mistakes can never be successful. But if he confesses and forsakes them, he gets another chance.
Proverbs 28:13 TLB

I let it all out; I said, "I'll make a clean breast of my failures to GOD." Suddenly the pressure was gone—my guilt dissolved, my sin disappeared.
Psalm 32:5 THE MESSAGE

He is so rich in kindness that he purchased our freedom through the blood of his Son, and our sins are forgiven.
Ephesians 1:7 NLT

I, the LORD, invite you to come and talk it over. Your sins are scarlet red, but they will be whiter than snow or wool. Isaiah 1:18 CEV

True repentance has a double aspect; it looks upon things past with a weeping eye, and upon the future with a watchful eye.
Robert Smith

Years of repentance are necessary in order to blot out a sin in the eyes of men, but one tear of repentance suffices with God.
French Proverb

We are certain that there is forgiveness, because there is a gospel, and the very essence of the gospel lies in the proclamation of the pardon of sin.
C. H. Spurgeon

As a child of God you are no longer a slave to sin.
Kay Arthur

I think that if God forgives us we must forgive ourselves. C. S. Lewis

It is the duty of nations as well as of men to own their dependence upon the overruling power of God . . . and to recognize the sublime truth announced in the Holy Scriptures and proven by all history, that those nations only are blessed whose God is the Lord.
Abraham Lincoln

The Gobbler Called Greed

He said to them, "Beware, and be on your guard against every form of greed; for not even when one has an abundance does his life consist of his possessions."

Luke 12:15 NASB

The Story Behind What Jesus Said

The voice came out of the crowd: "Teacher, tell my brother to divide the family inheritance with me." Few things divide families quicker than an inheritance. Since many rabbis often served as arbitrators for such disputes, the man in the crowd wanted Jesus to set things straight. Jesus refused. He had not come to be a judge in civil matters, but that didn't mean that he didn't have something to say.

Jesus shed light on the true problem, which was greed, not fairness. He gave a sharp warning that a constant guard must be kept against every form of greed. Life was not measured in possessions. The important things could not be counted because they were spiritual in nature.

On April 15, 1912, the "unsinkable" *Titanic* sank in the north Atlantic, taking with it over fifteen hundred people. A dozen millionaires were among those who drowned. One survivor, Major A. H. Peuchen, left over three hundred thousand dollars in money and jewels in his cabin. He said, "The money seemed a mockery at that time. I picked up three oranges instead."

Greed is an unrelenting temptation. Oak Island off Nova Scotia holds a treasure that people have been trying to retrieve since 1795. Several have died in the process. The treasure remains untouched, protected by a series of ingenious traps.

Money, possessions, and prosperity are not bad in and of themselves. The Bible does not speak against wealth, but it does make clear the sin of greed and the price that comes with it. Your life is not measured in dollars, acreage, stocks, or any other means of judging wealth. Life is measured in love and spirituality. Money is a tool and nothing more.

One Final Thought

Abundance and wealth may buy many things, but they cannot, by themselves, purchase contentment. It is far better to count blessings than dollars, to accumulate respect and love than gold.

A simple life in the Fear-of-GOD is better than a rich life with a ton of headaches.

Proverbs 15:16 THE MESSAGE

If you feel you must brag, then have enough sense to brag about worshiping me, the LORD. What I like best is showing kindness, justice, and mercy to everyone on earth.

Jeremiah 9:24 CEV

Keep your lives free from the love of money, and be satisfied with what you have. God has said, "I will never leave you; I will never forget you."

Hebrews 13:5 NCV

The love of money is a root of all kinds of evil, for which some have strayed from the faith in their greediness, and pierced themselves through with many sorrows.

1 Timothy 6:10 NKJV

Those who love money will never have enough. How absurd to think that wealth brings true happiness!

Ecclesiastes 5:10 NLT

A greedy man brings trouble to his family, but he who hates bribes will live.

Proverbs 15:27 NIV

God only, and not wealth, maintains the world; riches merely make people proud and lazy.
Martin Luther

The god of greed is a cheat. His delights have the power to dazzle and excite but they can satisfy nobody.
John White

Too many people spend money they haven't earned to buy things they don't want, to impress people they don't like.
Will Rogers

Millionaires who laugh are rare. My experience is that wealth is apt to take the smiles away.
Andrew Carnegie

The poorest man I know is the man who has nothing but money.
John D. Rockefeller Jr.

There is nothing wrong with people possessing riches. The wrong comes when riches possess people.
Billy Graham

Gold is like sea water—the more one drinks of it, the thirstier one becomes.
Arthur Schopenhauer

A Useless Thing

Jesus said, "And which of you by being anxious can add a single hour to his span of life?"

Luke 12:25 ESV

The Story Behind What Jesus Said

Anxiety is self-torment, and it gripped the people who listened to Jesus. The word Jesus used means to "examine minutely," to stew over something. People dwelled on how and when their lives would end. Such thoughts ate at them, and such concerns swallowed up the better thoughts of life.

Jesus made sure his listeners understood that such anxiety was a destructive waste of time. No matter how anxious they became, no matter how much they troubled themselves over such things, it made no difference. Anxiety couldn't extend a life, put food on the table, or drive away disease. Anxiety made things worse. It was time they let go and let God deal with matters out of their reach.

When Ann Landers was writing her popular advice column, she received an average of ten thousand letters a month. When asked if she saw a trend in the letters, some problem that seemed more common than others, she replied that most of the letters dealt with some form of fear. People were afraid of losing health, wealth, and loved ones. In short, people were afraid of life itself.

Impossible is a hard word for many to swallow, and learning that some things are beyond your control is unnerving. No one can control aging, world events, or decisions of loved ones, and that is unsettling. People fall into anxiety; they worry, they fret, they even lose sleep. And when it is all over, nothing has changed.

Anxiety is the most useless thing in the world. Like worry, it achieves nothing good but can cause great harm. The solution is simple. Change what you can and leave the rest in God's hands.

One Final Thought

The opposite of anxiety is trust; not trust in self—good as that is—but trusting God's love and ability. Anxiety is useless; faith is everything.

God, who calls you, is faithful; he will do this.

1 Thessalonians 5:24 NLT

I know that I will live to see the LORD's goodness in this present life. Trust in the LORD. Have faith, do not despair. Trust in the LORD.

Psalm 27:13–14 GNT

Delight yourself in the LORD and he will give you the desires of your heart. Commit your way to the LORD; trust in him and he will do this.

Psalm 37:4–5 NIV

God faithfully keeps his promises. He called you to be partners with his Son Jesus Christ our Lord.

1 Corinthians 1:9 GOD'S WORD

Let us hold firmly to the hope that we have confessed, because we can trust God to do what he promised.

Hebrews 10:23 NCV

Commit your works to the LORD, and your thoughts will be established.

Proverbs 16:3 NKJV

Do not anticipate trouble, or worry about what may never happen. Keep in the sunlight.
Benjamin Franklin

Our whole life is taken up with anxiety for personal security, with preparations for living, so that we really never live at all.
Leo Tolstoy

When a train goes through a tunnel and the world gets dark, do you jump out? Of course not. You sit still and trust the engineer to get you through.
Corrie ten Boom

Pray and let God worry.
Martin Luther

If you spend your whole life waiting for the storm, you'll never enjoy the sunshine. Morris West

An undivided heart, which worships God alone and trusts him as it should, is raised above all anxiety for earthly wants.
J. C. Geikie

Oh, how great peace and quietness would he possess who should cut off all vain anxiety and place all his confidence in God.
Thomas à Kempis

Calculating Cost

Jesus said, "Is there anyone here who, planning to build a new house, doesn't first sit down and figure the cost so you'll know if you can complete it?"

Luke 14:28 THE MESSAGE

The Story Behind What Jesus Said

In A.D. 27, not many years before Jesus uttered these words, an amphitheater collapsed killing an estimated fifty thousand people. The badly built structure had taken the lives of those who believed everything to be fine. The tragedy is now too far removed to know who was to blame, but it appears that corners were cut.

Jesus gives words to what many know instinctively, that great accomplishment comes at great cost. That price might be paid out in time, sweat, or money. To follow Jesus was costly too, and he wanted his disciples to count the cost before continuing on. It takes dedication to be a follower—Jesus wanted to make certain that the disciples had considered the cost.

This is a spontaneous generation, with decisions about life, work, and family being made quickly and, sadly, with too little thought. Life is a test of commitment and dedication. Jobs are lost, marriages fail, and businesses go under because the cost was not counted beforehand.

The great buildings of this time, the fabulous structures of the past, all came to be because someone had a dream and commitment. The forty-mile-long Panama Canal forms a waterway between the Atlantic and Pacific oceans. It was the largest and most complex project of its day, taking ten years to complete, thousands of workers, and nearly $350 million. Every imaginable obstacle presented itself, including disease-carrying mosquitoes.

The impossible became a reality because the cost was counted and the work continued with determination. The same is true for your life. The cost must first be counted, and then determination summoned. That's when great things happen. You can count on it.

One Final Thought

Before you begin anything worthwhile, determine what it will cost you emotionally, physically, and financially. If the goal is worthwhile, push on without fear and never look back.

We desire that each one of you show the same diligence to the full assurance of hope until the end. Hebrews 6:11 NKJV

Do you not know that those who run in a race all run, but only one receives the prize? Run in such a way that you may win.

1 Corinthians 9:24 NASB

Don't lose a minute in building on what you've been given, complementing your basic faith with good character, spiritual understanding, alert discipline, passionate patience, reverent wonder, warm friendliness, and generous love.

2 Peter 1:5–7 THE MESSAGE

You must continue to believe this truth and stand in it firmly. Don't drift away from the assurance you received when you heard the Good News.

Colossians 1:23 NLT

Oh, that we might know the Lord! Let us press on to know him, and he will respond to us as surely as the coming of dawn or the rain of early spring.

Hosea 6:3 TLB

Never be lacking in zeal, but keep your spiritual fervor, serving the Lord.

Romans 12:11 NIV

Oh, Lord, you give us everything, at the price of an effort.
Leonardo da Vinci

There are very few who in their hearts do not believe in God, but what they will not do is give Him exclusive right of way. They are not ready to promise full allegiance to God alone.
D. L. Moody

I feel that, if I could live a thousand lives, I would like to live them all for Christ.
C. H. Spurgeon

Man finds it hard to get what he wants, because he does not want the best; God finds it hard to give, because He would give the best, and man will not take it.
George MacDonald

It is impossible for a man to despair who remembers that his Helper is omnipotent. Jeremy Taylor

Be inspired with the belief that life is a great and noble calling; not a mean and groveling thing that we are to shuffle through as we can, but an elevated and lofty destiny.
William E. Gladstone

Forgetting the Wrong Things

Then Jesus answered and said, "Were there not ten cleansed? But the nine— where are they?"

Luke 17:17 NASB

The Story Behind What Jesus Said

Leprosy was one of the worst diseases in biblical times. The term leprosy was applied to any significant skin disorder—some fatal, some not. Perhaps worse than the disease was the forced isolation every leper endured. They were not allowed contact with others, including friends and family. If someone approached they were required to cry out a warning, "Unclean! Unclean!"

Jesus encountered ten such heartrending people. They recognized him and begged, "Have mercy on us!" Jesus did, sending them to show themselves to the priests as required by Jewish law. While they traveled they were healed. What a remarkable event. Even more remarkable, however, is the fact that only one came back to say thank you.

A pastor stood in his harbor-side church and announced that "nine men were lost at sea." The congregation was aghast having not heard of the tragedy. Seeing the surprise on their faces he remarked, "Well, eleven of you asked me to pray for the safety of men going to sea; since only two asked me to give thanks, I just assumed . . ."

Gratitude is often desired but too seldom expressed. Jesus faced ingratitude on many occasions, such as the case of ten miraculously healed lepers. Only one could be troubled to come back and thank Christ for his new health.

Saying thank-you is more than a courtesy; it is a heart indicator. Some people go through life thinking they deserve all the good that comes their way, never considering that their good fortune is the result of God's goodness or someone's prayer. Such belief shows a calloused heart. God deserves all the praise you can give him. Never forget his goodness.

One Final Thought

Look around and you will see the many blessings God has given you. Take time today to say thank-you to the one who deserves all your praise.

Oh, give thanks to the LORD! Call upon his name; make known his deeds among the peoples! Psalm 105:1 NKJV

O our God, we thank you and praise your glorious name!
1 Chronicles 29:13 NLT

Make a joyful noise unto the LORD, all ye lands. Serve the LORD with gladness: come before his presence with singing. Know ye that the LORD he is God: it is he that hath made us, and not we ourselves.
Psalm 100:1–3 KJV

Let the peace of Christ rule in your hearts, since as members of one body you were called to peace. And be thankful.
Colossians 3:15 NIV

Whatever you do or say, let it be as a representative of the Lord Jesus, and come with him into the presence of God the Father to give him your thanks.
Colossians 3:17 TLB

Be thankful in all circumstances. This is what God wants from you in your life in union with Christ Jesus. 1 Thessalonians 5:18 GNT

This day and your life are God's gift to you: so give thanks and be joyful always!
Jim Beggs

Reflect upon your present blessing—of which every man has many—not on your past misfortunes, of which all men have some.
Charles Dickens

We have short memories in magnifying God's grace. Every blessing that God confers upon us perished through our carelessness, if we are not prompt and active in giving thanks.
John Calvin

Thanksgiving is the end of all human conduct, whether observed in words or works.
J. B. Lightfoot

The person who has stopped being thankful has fallen asleep in life.
Robert Louis Stevenson

Both gratitude for God's past and current mercies, as well as hope-filled expectation of His future mercy are the strongest motives to live for His glory.
Scott Meadows

Unexpected Destination

He said to him, "Truly I say to you, today you shall be with Me in Paradise."

Luke 23:43 NASB

The Story Behind What Jesus Said

The darkest hour of history took place twenty centuries ago at a place near Jerusalem. Roman guards had brutalized Jesus and nailed him to the rough wood of the cross. Crucifixion was a horrible execution. Shock, dehydration, blood loss, and suffocation slowly took the victim's life in long, excruciating moments. Breathing was difficult, and speaking was close to impossible.

Crucified at the same time as Jesus were two thieves—one on his right, one on his left. Both railed at him and mocked him until the pain became too much. One had a change of heart and said, "Jesus, remember me when you come into your kingdom." Jesus took time out from dying to promise the thief Paradise.

In that promise, Jesus said more than most see. The thief had not been one of his followers, was not religious, kind, thoughtful, or courteous. He was a thief, a man of violence dangerous enough for Roman leaders to hang him on a cross.

The thief was a last-minute convert, making a decision about Christ in the last hour of his life. From his point of view on the cross, the thief would not have seen a rabbi, a popular teacher, or respected leader hanging next to him. He would have seen a man battered beyond recognition, bloodied by cruelty, whipped to the edge of death. Yet he saw something. He saw the solution to his eternity. No matter how Jesus looked, he was still the Savior.

The thief made it his business to settle his future and found Jesus willing to listen. Jesus is still listening today, and he is tuned in to your voice. Tell him what's on your mind.

One Final Thought

You cannot bother Jesus with a request or catch him at a bad time. Jesus took time out of dying to meet one person's need. He has time for you.

Seek the Lord while you can find him. Call upon him now while he is near. Isaiah 55:6 TLB

I cried out to God with my voice—to God with my voice; and He gave ear to me.
Psalm 77:1 NKJV

What does it say? "The word is near you; it is in your mouth and in your heart," that is, the word of faith we are proclaiming: That if you confess with your mouth, "Jesus is Lord," and believe in your heart that God raised him from the dead, you will be saved.
Romans 10:8–9 NIV

Then if my people who are called by my name will humble themselves and pray and seek my face and turn from their wicked ways, I will hear from heaven and will forgive their sins and heal their land.
2 Chronicles 7:14 NLT

What other great nation has gods that are intimate with them the way GOD, our God, is with us, always ready to listen to us?
Deuteronomy 4:7 THE MESSAGE

You will call to me. You will come and pray to me, and I will hear you.
Jeremiah 29:12 GOD'S WORD

Prayer is not overcoming God's reluctance; it is laying hold of His highest willingness.

Archbishop Trench

Some people think God does not like to be troubled with our constant coming and asking. The way to trouble God is not to come at all.

D. L. Moody

Because God is the living God, he can hear; because he is a loving God, he will hear; because he is our covenant God, he has bound himself to hear.

Charles Spurgeon

In prayer it is better to have a heart without words than words without a heart.

John Bunyan

Nothing is too great and nothing is too small to commit into the hands of the Lord. A. W. Pink

All God's love and the fruits of it come to us as we are in Christ, and are one with him. Then in our passage to God again we must return all, and do all, to God in Christ.

Richard Sibbes

How comforting it is to know that the Father's face is, indeed, always turned toward us.

Mary Prince

Mistaken Identity

While they were saying all this, Jesus appeared to them and said, "Peace be with you." They thought they were seeing a ghost and were scared half to death.

Luke 24:36–37 THE MESSAGE

The Story Behind What Jesus Said

The most fundamental belief of Christians is that Christ died and rose from the dead. It is the foundation of the faith, and no doctrine is more important. Jesus told beforehand that he would die on the cross and then rise on the third day. It was hard for the disciples to believe. Who can blame them?

But Jesus did rise from the grave, and he appeared twelve times over a forty-day span. Each time he appeared, he did so physically, and each time he was met with astonishment. In one of the earliest appearances, the disciples were so stunned by the sight of the risen Jesus they assumed they were seeing a ghost. They couldn't believe their eyes.

Ralph Hodgson made a thought-provoking quip when he said, "Some things have to be believed to be seen." In today's world people have been taught to believe only that which they can see, only what they can touch. The problem is, they don't always see the truth. Just like the disciples, their minds can jump to erroneous conclusions, especially if the truth comes unexpectedly.

The skeptic in people often pushes away what they know to be true. It's something you've probably experienced. Believing often requires that you confront previous beliefs and see if they hold up to new truth. Too many are willing to believe in ghosts rather than a risen Savior. Skepticism may cause you to avoid reality because reality makes life-changing demands.

Jesus stands before your heart and your mind. Don't try to explain him away. Don't relegate him to the pages of history. See him. Embrace him. He is more real than most people can imagine.

One Final Thought

Most things are exactly as they appear, and this is true for the spiritual life. Jesus is everything he claimed to be. Believing that is everyone's choice—it's your choice.

If we are faithless, he remains faithful; he cannot deny Himself. 2 Timothy 2:13 NKJV

Without faith no one can please God. Anyone who comes to God must believe that he is real and that he rewards those who truly want to find him.
Hebrews 11:6 NCV

After his suffering, he showed himself to these men and gave many convincing proofs that he was alive. He appeared to them over a period of forty days and spoke about the kingdom of God.
Acts 1:3 NIV

People who aren't Christians can't understand these truths from God's Spirit.
1 Corinthians 2:14 NLT

I delivered to you first of all that which I also received: that Christ died for our sins according to the Scriptures, and that He was buried, and that He rose again the third day according to the Scriptures.
1 Corinthians 15:3–4 NKJV

Abraham never doubted. He believed God, for his faith and trust grew ever stronger, and he praised God for this blessing even before it happened. Romans 4:20 TLB

Don't worry about what you do not understand. Worry about what you do understand in the Bible but do not live by.
Corrie ten Boom

A man was meant to be doubtful about himself but undoubting about the truth. This has been exactly reversed.
G. K. Chesterton

Skepticism has not founded empires, established principles, or changed the word's heart. The great doers of history have always been men of faith.
Edwin Hubbel Chapin

Most of our so-called reasoning consists in finding arguments for going on believing as we already do.
James Harvey Robinson

We know the truth, not only by reason, but also by heart. Blaise Pascal

None but the Lord himself can afford us any help from the awful workings of unbelief, doubtings, carnal fears, murmurings. Thank God one day we will be done forever with "unbelief."
Arthur W. Pink

151

Who Stirred Up the Storm?

He said to them, "See My hands and My feet, that it is I Myself; touch Me and see, for a spirit does not have flesh and bones as you see that I have."

Luke 24:39 NASB

The Story Behind What Jesus Said

As thoughts of ghosts haunted the minds of the disciples, the resurrected Jesus made an effort to comfort them. His sudden appearance in a closed room had shocked the disciples beyond words, and Jesus knew it. What does one do with a roomful of terrified followers?

Jesus' solution was to offer his very body as evidence. If seeing wasn't believing, then maybe touching was. In that crowded upper room, Jesus extended an invitation: "Touch me." Imagine him standing there with a wide smile on his face and his hands extended before him. Jesus was making it as easy and as personal as possible for the disciples to put away ghostly thoughts and embrace the truth of the resurrection. Their eyes were open; they needed to open their hearts.

Each adult has three pounds of gray matter called a brain. It's a complex organ, a mass of one hundred billion nerve cells. That softball-size structure governs your breathing, sleeping, speaking, walking, writing, thinking, and everything else you do. When the brain encounters something out of the ordinary, it naturally tries to explain it.

In biblical imagery, the heart is as important as the brain. While the brain might deal with the facts, the heart deals with truth. Some things you know to be true even if you cannot make a list of reasons why.

Seeing the world—seeing Christ—through the eyes of the intellect is a good thing. Seeing the world with the eyes of the heart is life changing. It is in the heart that truth resides and works in your lives. To know something intellectually is admirable, but to experience it you must also know it in your heart.

One Final Thought

Jesus made the effort to prove himself to the disciples, and they believed. Jesus works to make himself known to you. What does your heart tell you?

I will praise You, O LORD, with my whole heart; I will tell of all Your marvelous works.

Psalm 9:1 NKJV

God, who said, "Light shall shine out of darkness," is the One who has shone in our hearts to give the Light of the knowledge of the glory of God in the face of Christ.

2 Corinthians 4:6 NASB

One of those listening was a woman named Lydia, a dealer in purple cloth from the city of Thyatira, who was a worshiper of God. The Lord opened her heart to respond to Paul's message.

Acts 16:14 NIV

The Lord said to Samuel, "Don't judge by a man's face or height, for this is not the one. I don't make decisions the way you do! Men judge by outward appearance, but I look at a man's thoughts and intentions."

1 Samuel 16:7 TLB

I, the LORD, look into a person's heart and test the mind. So I can decide what each one deserves; I can give each one the right payment for what he does.

Jeremiah 17:10 NCV

You must love the LORD your God with all your heart, all your soul, and all your strength. Deuteronomy 6:5 NLT

To my God a heart of flame; to my fellow men a heart of love; to myself a heart of steel.
Saint Augustine

It is faith, and not reason, which impels men to action. . . . Intelligence is content to point out the road, but never drives us along it.
Alexis Carrel

It is the heart which perceives God and not the reason.
Blaise Pascal

Faith doesn't wait until it understands; in that case it wouldn't be faith.
Vance Havner

Only the heart knows how to find what is precious. Fyodor Dostoevsky

Throw your heart over the fence and the rest will follow.
Norman Vincent Peale

Some like to understand what they believe in. Others like to believe in what they understand.
Saint Stanislaus

Living a Level Above

Jesus said, "God is spirit, and those who worship Him must worship in spirit and truth."

John 4:24 NASB

The Story Behind What Jesus Said

Prejudice is not new. The Samaritans lived in central Palestine and were a mix of transplanted Assyrians and Jews. Many Jews hated them. Jews who walked across Samaritan soil would shake the dust from their sandals. The Samaritans returned the hatred. That is what makes this passage so interesting.

Jesus sat by a well when a Samaritan woman approached. She arrived in the middle of the day rather than in the morning when other women from the village would have drawn water. Her immoral behavior had made her an outcast. Jesus struck up a conversation. That act was stunning. He broke all social rules to make sure this woman understood that even she could worship God in spirit and truth.

The tiny words make the difference. After a proposal of marriage, the little words yes and no make a big difference. Jesus uses a word that is easy to overlook: those. After a discussion of what was the correct way to worship, Jesus got to the heart of the matter. "Those who worship him," he said. Those who worship God. No mention of Jews. No mention of Samaritans. Just "those who worship."

It was an unlikely conversation. First, Samaritans didn't talk to Jews. Women didn't talk to men who were not family. And certainly immoral people didn't chat with religious teachers. Yet there they were, a male Jew conversing with a female Samaritan and talking about how to worship God.

The scene is simple but beautiful. It doesn't matter who you are, what people think of you, or what you've done in the past, God is ready to be worshiped by those who do so in spirit and truth.

One Final Thought

Problems, shortcomings, and sad personal history can be resolved with sincere and regular worship. That's true for everyone. Get reacquainted with God—he is waiting to hear from you.

Bow down and worship the LORD our Creator! The LORD is our God, and we are his people, the sheep he takes care of in his own pasture. Listen to God's voice today!

Psalm 95:6–7 CEV

Take your everyday, ordinary life—your sleeping, eating, going-to-work, and walking-around life—and place it before God as an offering.

Romans 12:1 THE MESSAGE

I live in a high and holy place, but also with him who is contrite and lowly in spirit.

Isaiah 57:15 NIV

You must honor God with your body.

1 Corinthians 6:20 NLT

When I think of the wisdom and scope of his plan, I fall down on my knees and pray to the Father . . . that out of his glorious, unlimited resources he will give you the mighty inner strengthening of his Holy Spirit.

Ephesians 3:14–16 TLB

Exalt the LORD our God, and worship at His footstool—He is holy. Psalm 99:5 NKJV

To worship is to quicken the conscience by the holiness of God, to feed the mind with the truth of God, to purge the imagination by the beauty of God, to open the heart to the love of God, to devote the will to the purpose of God.
William Temple

We would know, O God our Father, that Thou art near us and beside us; that Thou dost love us and that Thou are concerned about all our affairs. May we become aware of Thy companionship, of Him who walks beside us.
Peter Marshall

Worship is the highest and noblest activity of which man, by the grace of God, is capable. John Stott

God is not moved or impressed with our worship until our hearts are moved and impressed by him.
Kelly Sparks

You do not go to church to hear a sermon. You go to church to worship God and to serve him in the fellowship of other Christians.
Billy Graham

Miracles and Orders

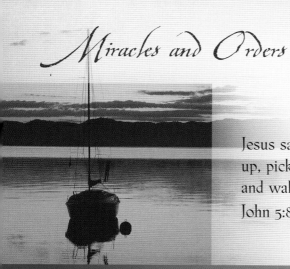

Jesus said to him, "Get up, pick up your pallet and walk."

John 5:8 NASB

The Story Behind What Jesus Said

In Jerusalem for one of the many annual feasts, Christ entered an area by a pool. The name of the pool was Bethesda, which means "House of Mercy." Many believed that an angel would descend from heaven and stir up the waters. If an ill person were to step into the pool at that time a healing would take place.

Many would gather around the pool waiting for the waters to be stirred. One such man had been paralyzed for thirty-eight years, unable to make it to the pool in time. Jesus asked, "Do you wish to get well?" Odd question, but the answer was a quick "Yes." A moment later the man could stand, walk, and even carry his bed.

Jesus began with a strange question: "Do you want to get well?" Then the strange command: "Get up, pick up your pallet and walk." Thirty-eight years of paralysis came down to a moment of belief. What went through the man's mind? Whatever it was, he had the courage to try.

Courage of faith, courage of belief, and courage to try have changed the world. There came a time for Noah to cut the first piece of wood and drive the first nail in the ark. Miracles are works of God that are rooted in our faith.

It takes courage to have enough faith to stand up after thirty-eight years of paralysis. It takes faith to face the future with confidence, to work in the present with authority, and to gleefully release the past to the past. What should you do if Jesus tells you to do something, even the unexpected? Do it. Don't let fear of failure hold you back.

One Final Thought

Fear is an anchor. You may not see it, but it's there. Courage is freedom to soar. Courage means believing that there are more solutions than problems. Be empowered by God.

He gives power to the weak, and to those who have no might He increases strength.

Isaiah 40:29 NKJV

I will sing about your strength, my God, and I will celebrate because of your love. You are my fortress, my place of protection in times of trouble. I will sing your praises! You are my mighty fortress, and you love me.

Psalm 59:16–17 CEV

He said to me, "My grace is sufficient for you, for my power is made perfect in weakness." Therefore I will boast all the more gladly about my weaknesses, so that Christ's power may rest on me.

2 Corinthians 12:9 NIV

Encourage those who are afraid. Tell them, "Be strong, fear not, for your God is coming to destroy your enemies. He is coming to save you."

Isaiah 35:4 TLB

The LORD is my strength and my song; he has become my victory. He is my God, and I will praise him; he is my father's God, and I will exalt him!

Exodus 15:2 NLT

Be strong in the Lord, and in the power of his might. Ephesians 6:10 KJV

God's gifts put man's best dreams to shame.
Elizabeth Barrett Browning

In our weakness, God empowers. In our moments of doubt, God assures. We fall, He lifts us up, and when we see, He dries our tears. God gives freely to those who call upon him.
Mary Prince

Our heavenly Father never takes anything from his children unless he means to give them something better.
George Müller

We are never stronger than the moment when we admit we are weak.
Beth Moore

Try . . . take the risk . . . in the doing there is freedom! Colleen Townsend Evans

Crowds of people— sick, blind, lame, and paralyzed—all waiting— hoping—that they would be healed. Into this assembly of desperate, heartweary, suffering people came Jesus. . . . He went over and healed him instantly; the love and concern of Jesus Christ for someone, who had no one.
Joan Winmill Brown

Bubbling Over

Jesus said, "He who believes in Me, as the Scripture said, 'From his innermost being will flow rivers of living water.'"

John 7:38 NASB

The Story Behind What Jesus Said

During one of the great feasts of Israel, Jesus stood and made a startling announcement. It was the last day of the Feast of Tabernacles, an eight-day celebration of God's protection of the Hebrews during their forty years of wilderness wanderings. Each day the priest would make a formal march to the spring of Gihon, fill a gold pitcher with water, return to the temple, and pour it over the altar. It was a reminder of God's miraculous provision of water from a dry rock.

Water from a desert rock is impossible except with God. Jesus used the same symbolism to invite the crowds to place their belief in him and become sources of living water for others.

Water is life. Water makes up fifty to ninety percent of any animal's weight. Without water there would be no life. No one knows this better than those who live in arid areas. Such desert conditions were known to the people of Jesus' time. Their history included a four-decade wilderness wandering. Talk of water was important talk.

Jesus likened himself to life-giving water but then went the next step. Not only is he the source of eternal life, but those who believe in him become conduits of truth to the lives of others. Jesus was speaking of the Holy Spirit, the third person of the Trinity.

What is on the inside of people becomes apparent to others. Like the ancient Roman aqueducts that carried thirty-eight million gallons of water to Rome each day (some are still used today), you can carry the spiritual life to others by letting truth flow through you. The key is belief in Jesus.

One Final Thought

Jesus threw wide the door of invitation and made a promise that belief in him led to life and life-giving influence. Let Jesus in and let the truth out.

Just as you received Christ Jesus as Lord, continue to live in him, rooted and built up in him, strengthened in the faith as you were taught, and overflowing with thankfulness.

Colossians 2:6–7 NIV

The LORD will guide you continually, and satisfy your soul in drought, and strengthen your bones; you shall be like a watered garden, and like a spring of water, whose waters do not fail.

Isaiah 58:11 NKJV

Since we live by the Spirit, let us keep in step with the Spirit.

Galatians 5:25 NIV

You are the Fountain of life; our light is from your light. Pour out your unfailing love on those who know you!

Psalm 36:9–10 TLB

The Kingdom of God is not a matter of what we eat or drink, but of living a life of goodness and peace and joy in the Holy Spirit.

Romans 14:17 NLT

All of them drank the same spiritual drink. They drank from the spiritual rock that went with them, and that rock was Christ.

1 Corinthians 10:4 GOD'S WORD

The Spirit dwelling and working in believers is as a fountain of living running water, out of which plentiful streams flow, cooling and cleansing as water, mollifying and moistening as water, making them fruitful, and others joyful.
Matthew Henry

The serene beauty of a holy life is the most powerful influence in the world next to the power of God.
Blaise Pascal

Every time we say, "I believe in the Holy Spirit," we mean that we believe that there is a living God able and willing to enter human personality and change it.
J. B. Philips

We can influence others as much as God has influenced us. Bobbie-Jean Merck

Happy the man whose words come from the Holy Spirit and not from himself.
Saint Anthony of Padua

I will find in every person the facet of the Lord's loveliness that only he or she can uniquely reflect.
Joni Eareckson Tada

Freedom Never Travels Alone

Jesus said, "And you will know the truth, and the truth will make you free."

John 8:32 NASB

The Story Behind What Jesus Said

"If you continue in my word, then you are truly disciples of mine," Jesus said to a group of hearers who "believed in him." Belief needed to become lifestyle, not mere mental agreement. Such a commitment, Jesus promised, would bring truth, and truth would bring freedom.

Many that were professing belief in Jesus would soon pick up rocks to stone him. As long as he taught things that were easy to believe and didn't contradict previously held assumptions, then the crowd was with Jesus, but when he taught the hard truths, truths that required change, they balked. Truth recognized changed nothing; truth accepted changed everything. Freedom was a door that only truth could open.

Truth is sweet. It is also sharp. It can be pleasing to hear, uplifting to know, and encouraging to feel in the soul; it can also slice deep into preconceived ideas and long-held desires. To know truth, the mind must be willing not only to hear, but to accept.

Four hundred years before Christ a man named Diogenes wandered around Athens carrying a lantern in his hand—during the daytime. He would approach people, lift the lamp, and say, "I am looking for an honest man." The story has it that he never found one.

Honesty is truth's companion. For most people, basic honesty is easy. Being honest with yourself, however, is much more difficult. It is honesty that allows people to see the truth, and that truth sets them free. Be honest with yourself, about yourself. Only then can you be honest with God. Then you will have the truth and that truth will set you free.

One Final Thought

To know freedom, you must know the truth; to know the truth, you must know Christ; to know Christ, you must also honestly know yourself.

Guide me in your truth, and teach me, my God, my Savior. I trust you all day long.

Psalm 25:5 NCV

You have been called to live in freedom—not freedom to satisfy your sinful nature, but freedom to serve one another in love.

Galatians 5:13 NLT

However, when He, the Spirit of truth, has come, He will guide you into all truth; for He will not speak on His own authority, but whatever He hears He will speak; and He will tell you things to come.

John 16:13 NKJV

You have received the Holy Spirit and he lives within you, in your hearts, so that you don't need anyone to teach you what is right. For he teaches you all things, and he is the Truth, and no liar; and so, just as he has said, you must live in Christ, never to depart from him.

1 John 2:27 TLB

I know that you heard about him, and you are in him, so you were taught the truth that is in Jesus.

Ephesians 4:21 NCV

They devoted themselves to the apostles' teaching and to the fellowship, to the breaking of bread and to prayer.

Acts 2:42 NIV

If any man can convince me and bring home to me that I do not think or act aright, gladly will I change; for I search after truth, by which man never yet was harmed. But he is harmed who abideth on still in his deception and ignorance.

Marcus Aurelius Antoninus

Where I found truth, there found I my God, who is the truth itself.

Saint Augustine

Truth does not change because it is, or is not, believed by a majority of the people.

Giordano Bruno

Rather than love, than money, than fame, give me truth. Henry David Thoreau

Christ is the key which unlocks the golden doors into the temple of Divine truth.

A. W. Pink

We find freedom when we find God; we lose it when we lose him.

Paul E. Scherer

Where Everybody Knows Your Name

Jesus said, "My sheep know my voice, and I know them. They follow me."

John 10:27 CEV

The Story Behind What Jesus Said

Very few people in our culture can understand the relationship a shepherd has with his flock. A good shepherd provides direction, leadership, and protection for the sheep. The shepherd can identify individual sheep, knowing the health, strength, and weakness of each one. The sheep grow accustomed to the shepherd, trusting his presence and even learning to recognize his voice. Good sheep follow the shepherd—a good shepherd gives them reason to.

Although a carpenter by training, Jesus compared himself to a shepherd. Nothing in the ancient world could portray his love for his followers like that of a good shepherd who cares for the sheep in his charge. As sheep know their shepherd's voice, so Christians are to know their Savior's voice.

One of the goals of computer science is to create a computer that recognizes the human voice. Some headway has been made, but to date, voice recognition software is inaccurate and difficult to use. Those programs that work the best have to be "trained" to identify the speech patterns and pronunciations of the user. Even then, they are wrong much of the time.

The human ear, however, is a highly tuned instrument, able to easily distinguish one person from another. Family members can recognize each other at great distance over the phone, even if the speaker tries to disguise his or her voice. It's an amazing ability.

Christians are connected to Christ in a remarkable way. Spiritually, it is as if they can hear his voice and recognize it immediately. This kind of relationship is not academic, it is personal. That's how Jesus intended it for you—close and personal. Listening is still required. Responding is the proper and natural thing to do.

One Final Thought

You have a spiritual ear. Does Jesus speak audibly to you? Probably not—he speaks a great deal louder than that. Tune in and listen to the voice of Jesus.

"I will set up shepherds over them who will feed them; and they shall fear no more, nor be dismayed, nor shall they be lacking," says the LORD. Jeremiah 23:4 NKJV

He will stand to lead his flock with the LORD's strength, in the majesty of the name of the LORD his God. Then his people will live there undisturbed, for he will be highly honored all around the world. Micah 5:4 NLT

If you hear my voice and open the door, I will come in and eat with you, and you will eat with me. Revelation 3:20 NCV

The Lord is my shepherd; I shall not want. He maketh me to lie down in green pastures: he leadeth me beside the still waters. He restoreth my soul: he leadeth me in the paths of righteousness for his name's sake. Psalm 23:1–3 KJV

The Lord knows those who are his. 2 Timothy 2:19 NIV

I am the Good Shepherd and know my own sheep, and they know me, just as my Father knows me and I know the Father; and I lay down my life for the sheep. John 10:14–15 TLB

Savior, like a shepherd lead us; much we need Thy tender care; in Thy pleasant pastures feed us; for our use Thy folds prepare: Blessed Jesus, blessed Jesus, Thou has bought us, Thine we are; blessed Jesus, blessed Jesus, Thou hast bought us, Thine we are.
Dorothy A. Thrupp

The love of Christ is like the blue sky, into which you may see clearly, but the real vastness of which you cannot measure.
Robert Murray McCheyne

The great Shepherd of the sheep takes wonderful care of the flock and of all that belong to it.
Matthew Henry

Jesus does not give recipes that show the way to God as other teachers of religion do. He is himself the way.
Karl Barth

No one has a right to claim to be one of Christ's sheep if he or she lives in willful, persistent, open disobedience, and refuses to do something about it. Just as there are false shepherds, so there are goats who try to pass for sheep.
Warren Wiersbe

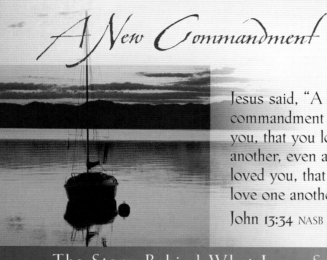

A New Commandment

Jesus said, "A new commandment I give to you, that you love one another, even as I have loved you, that you also love one another.

John 13:34 NASB

The Story Behind What Jesus Said

Moses stood on the mountaintop and received the Law from God. The Law was summed up in the Ten Commandments. Fifteen hundred years later, Jesus made a bold statement. "A new commandment I give to you." Those were weighted words. To the Jewish ear they would have sounded strange and out of place. Only God could add to the commandments.

Jesus indeed gave another commandment—a mandate to love. Not just any love given in any fashion, but a love that reflected his own. The command was to love one another in the same fashion and to the extreme extent that he had loved. He set the bar higher than it had ever been set before.

Uniforms are everywhere. Police officers are identified by the uniform they wear. Sports teams are identified by certain colors and designs. The uniform worn by those who follow Christ is love. "People will know you are my disciples," Jesus added, "by the way you love one another." What distinguished the followers of Christ was not the clothing they wore, the accent they had, or the way they wore their hair. People identified them with Christ because of the manner of their love.

Love cannot be seen. It has no substance, no color, no aroma, nothing in its nature to make it noticeable. Love is immeasurable. There is no such thing as a gallon of love. Love, however, can be seen in action, in words, in patience, and in a hundred other ways in which Christ is imitated.

Like electricity, love must flow between two points: you and someone else. Love is not a feeling, it is a chosen expression.

One Final Thought

Your most powerful weapon is love. It is also your most useful tool. The love you show will identify you with Christ more than the name of any church denomination.

Stop being angry and don't try to take revenge.
I am the LORD, and I command you to love
others as much as you love yourself.
Leviticus 19:18 CEV

The person who refuses to
love doesn't know the first
thing about God, because
God is love—so you can't
know him if you don't love.
1 John 4:8 THE MESSAGE

Therefore be imitators
of God as dear children.
And walk in love, as
Christ also has loved us.
Ephesians 5:1–2 NKJV

Make me truly happy by
agreeing wholeheartedly
with each other, loving
one another, and working
together with one heart
and purpose.
Philippians 2:2 NLT

If I speak in the
tongues of men and
of angels, but have
not love, I am only a
resounding gong or
a clanging cymbal.
1 Corinthians 13:1 NIV

May the Lord make your love to grow and
overflow to each other and to everyone
else, just as our love does toward you.
1 Thessalonians 3:12 TLB

Anybody can be a heart specialist. The only requirement is loving somebody.
Angie Papadakis

Love is not blind— it sees more, not less. But because it sees more, it is willing to see less.
Rabbi Julius Gordon

To love is to will the good of another.
Saint Thomas Aquinas

Love is always open arms. With arms open you allow love to come and go as it will, freely, for it'll do so anyway. If you close your arms about love, you'll find you are left only holding yourself.
Leo Buscaglia

The loneliest place in the world is the human heart when love is absent. E. C. McKenzie

You will find, as you look back upon your life, that the moments when you really lived are the moments when you have done things in the spirit of love.
Henry Drummond

Love doesn't just sit there like a stone, it has to be made, like bread; remade all the time, made new.
Ursula K. Le Guin

179

Branching Out

Jesus said, "I am the vine, you are the branches; he who abides in Me and I in him, he bears much fruit, for apart from Me you can do nothing."

John 15:5 NASB

The Story Behind What Jesus Said

If Jesus were like any other teacher, then his words would carry no more weight than the hundreds that came before and after. But Jesus is different. Two thousand years later, his words are as life altering as they were the moment he uttered them.

What makes Jesus different is his bond to his followers. He taught that there was a mutual abiding of him in them, and they in him. Using the image of a grape plant, he taught that he was the vine and his followers were the branches. They could not produce the "fruit" without being securely attached to him. He would provide everything they needed to make a difference in their lives and in the world.

Today millions of computers sit atop desks throughout the world. Without traveling to the most remote parts of the planet it is difficult to find someone who hasn't used a computer. No matter how powerful the computer, it still must have certain peripherals to be used by humans. Without a keyboard, mouse, monitor, and printer, the computer is little more than an expensive paperweight. But with those things connected, wonderful things can be done.

Your relationship with Christ is the same. You may have many skills and abilities, but they cannot reach their potential without connecting to the divine. Unlike the computer, there are no cables linking you to Jesus. That link begins in the mind, centers in the heart, and connects through the soul. No one is complete until he or she has connected to Christ. Faith is more than belief, it is connection. The choice to connect rests with the individual. The decision is yours. Are you connected?

One Final Thought

Purpose, strength, power, hope, and meaningful existence begin with and flow through Jesus. He is the divine conduit of all things good and meaningful. Make the connection.

We must listen very carefully to the truths we have heard, or we may drift away from them.
Hebrews 2:1 TLB

I have died, but Christ lives in me. And I now live by faith in the Son of God, who loved me and gave his life for me.
Galatians 2:20 CEV

Let that abide in you which you heard from the beginning. If what you heard from the beginning abides in you, you also will abide in the Son and in the Father. And this is the promise that He has promised us—eternal life.
1 John 2:24–25 NKJV

Anyone who runs ahead and does not continue in the teaching of Christ does not have God; whoever continues in the teaching has both the Father and the Son.
2 John 1:9 NIV

I am the vine. You are the branches. Those who live in me while I live in them will produce a lot of fruit. But you can't produce anything without me.
John 15:5 GOD'S WORD

I pray that Christ will be more and more at home in your hearts as you trust in him. May your roots go down deep into the soil of God's marvelous love. Ephesians 3:17 NLT

Abide in me says Jesus. Cling to me. Stick fast to me. Live the life of close and intimate communion with me. Get nearer to me. Roll every burden on me. Cast your whole weight on me. Never let go your hold on me for a moment. Be, as it were, rooted and planted in me. Do this and I will never fail you. I will ever abide in you.
J. C. Ryle

Abide in Jesus, the sinless one—which means, give up all of self and its life, and dwell in God's will and rest in his strength.
Andrew Murray

Watch against lip religion. Above all abide in Christ and he will abide in you.
Robert Murray McCheyne

You have nothing to do in life except to live in union with Christ. Rufus Mosely

He who leans only upon Christ, lives the highest, choicest, safest, and sweetest life.
Thomas Brooks

Our union with Christ is a living union, so we may bear fruit; a loving union, so that we may enjoy Him; and a lasting union, so that we need not be afraid.
Warren Wiersbe

Not Seeing Is Believing

Jesus said to him, "Because you have seen Me, have you believed? Blessed are they who did not see, and yet believed."

John 20:29 NASB

The Story Behind What Jesus Said

Thomas has a nickname— "doubting" Thomas. He's called that because of something that happened after Christ's resurrection. For unknown reasons, Thomas was not with the other disciples when Jesus appeared to them. Whatever errand kept him away caused him to miss one of the first appearances of the resurrected Christ. When he returned the others were overjoyed at what they had experienced and told Thomas the tale. Thomas wasn't convinced. "Unless I see the wound in his side and the nail-scars in his hand, I won't believe."

Jesus appeared again, this time when Thomas was present. He presented his wounded hands and side. Thomas didn't need to touch—he fell to his knees and said, "My Lord and my God."

"Seeing is believing," some have said. Jesus overturned that attitude. Not seeing is believing, he said. Someone remarked, "Faith sees the invisible, believes the incredible, and receives the impossible." You needn't see electricity to use its power; you don't have to see digestion work to know that you need food to survive.

Jesus said that believing by sight is a blessing and that a greater blessing is reserved for those who believe without seeing. The proofs for the resurrection are many, but they mean nothing to those who choose not to believe; they mean everything to those who decide to believe.

An unknown thinker said, "Faith is to believe what we do not see; and the reward of this faith is to see what we believe." Some demand that Christ appear to them before entrusting their lives to him. For many, seeing with their heart is more convincing than seeing with their eyes. The heart sees more than the eyes.

One Final Thought

Your five physical senses tell you about the world, but your spiritual sense tells you about truth, trust, belief, and faith. Listen to that spiritual voice; it may be Jesus.

The things which are seen are temporary, but the things which are not seen are eternal.

2 Corinthians 4:18 NKJV

I pray that God, who gives you hope, will keep you happy and full of peace as you believe in him. May you overflow with hope through the power of the Holy Spirit.

Romans 15:13 NLT

Let us run with endurance the race that is set before us, fixing our eyes on Jesus, the author and perfecter of faith.

Hebrews 12:1 NASB

We can see and understand only a little about God now, as if we were peering at his reflection in a poor mirror; but someday we are going to see him in his completeness, face to face.

1 Corinthians 13:12 TLB

Even though you do not see him now, you believe in him and are filled with an inexpressible and glorious joy.

1 Peter 1:8 NIV

If we hope for something we already see, it's not really hope. Who hopes for what can be seen? But if we hope for what we don't see, we eagerly wait for it with perseverance. Romans 8:24b–25 GOD'S WORD

A little faith will bring your soul to heaven; a great faith will bring heaven to your soul.
C. H. Spurgeon

Perhaps the transformation of the disciples of Jesus is the greatest evidence of all for the resurrection.
John Stott

God does not expect us to submit our faith to him without reason, but the very limits of reason make faith a necessity.
Saint Augustine

Belief consists in accepting the affirmations of the soul; unbelief, in denying them.
Ralph Waldo Emerson

Christ has turned all our sunsets into dawns. Clement of Alexander

I am not moved by what I see. I am not moved by what I feel. I am moved only by what I believe.
Smith Wigglesworth

When we believe in nothing, we open the doors to believing anything.
David Wells

Front to Back

Jesus said, "I am Alpha and Omega, the first and the last, the beginning and the end."

Revelation 22:13 CEV

The Story Behind What Jesus Said

Revelation is a book about the future. It is filled with prophecies yet to happen. It also reveals important information about the nature of Christ. The apostle John has a long, detailed, and complicated vision where the future is revealed. More important, Christ is described in amazing ways, emphasizing his unique qualities.

During this vision, Jesus describes himself as the Alpha and Omega—the first and the last letters of the Greek alphabet. Like all New Testament books, Revelation was written in Greek. If Jesus were speaking in English, he would have said, "I am the *A* and the *Z*." Jesus is the beginning, the middle, and he encompasses the end. Jesus' point was that all things are summed up in him.

Everything has a beginning and an end. Life is the journey between those two points. Jesus is before the beginning and has no end. All that the universe is, all that time contains, is contained in him. Often, people view Jesus just as he was during his three-year ministry, but he is far beyond that.

Through life everyone learns that he or she has shortcomings, weaknesses, and faults. You may be shouldering such thoughts now. Courage comes from knowing that you do not journey through this life alone—you have someone to guide you in.

When large ships sail into port, they take aboard a harbor pilot. The ship's captain may have safely guided the ship across the wide sea, but he needs help from one who knows the harbor better than he. Jesus knows your harbor. The entire world and all of time are his port. It makes sense to have someone aboard who knows everything from beginning to end.

One Final Thought

Jesus is there to help you pilot your ship. He knows where you've been, and he knows what lies ahead. Let him have a chance at the wheel.

The mind of man plans his way, but the LORD directs his steps. Proverbs 16:9 NASB

This great God is our God forever and ever. He will be our guide until we die.
Psalm 48:14 TLB

I'll take the hand of those who don't know the way, who can't see where they're going. I'll be a personal guide to them, directing them through unknown country. I'll be right there to show them what roads to take, make sure they don't fall into the ditch.
Isaiah 42:16 THE MESSAGE

As it is written: "Eye has not seen, nor ear heard, nor have entered into the heart of man the things which God has prepared for those who love Him."
1 Corinthians 2:9 NKJV

The Lamb who stands in front of the throne will be their Shepherd. He will lead them to the springs of life-giving water. And God will wipe away all their tears.
Revelation 7:17 NLT

Since you are my rock and my fortress, for the sake of your name lead and guide me.
Psalm 31:3 NIV

I recognized that our Lord had caused me to run aground at this place so that I might establish a settlement here. And so many things came to hand here that the disaster was a blessing in disguise.
Christopher Columbus

God moves in a mysterious way His wonders to perform; He plants His footsteps in the sea, And rides upon the storm.
William Cowper

Knowing that I am not the one in control gives great encouragement. Knowing the one who is in control is everything.
Alexander Michael

Submit each day to God, knowing that he is God over all your tomorrows. Kay Arthur

I have lived a long time and the longer I live the more convincing proofs I see that God governs in the affairs of men.
Benjamin Franklin

We serve a gracious Master who knows how to overrule even our mistakes to his glory and our own advantage.
John Newton